The Writing

Also by David Lodge

THE WRITING GAME

A Comedy

David Lodge

Secker & Warburg
London

First published in 1991 by
Martin Secker & Warburg Limited
an imprint of Reed Consumer Books Ltd
Michelin House, 81 Fulham Road, London SW3 6RB
and Auckland, Melbourne, Singapore and Toronto

Reprinted 1991, 1994

A CIP catalogue record for this book
is available from the British Library
ISBN 0 436 25666 5

Set in 10 point Plantin
by CentraCet, Cambridge
Printed and bound in Great Britain
by Cox & Wyman Ltd, Reading, Berkshire

The Writing Game was first performed at the Birmingham Repertory Theatre on 12 May 1990. It was directed by John Adams and designed by Roger Butlin, with lighting by Mark Pritchard. The cast was as follows:

JEREMY DEANE John Webb
LEO RAFKIN Lou Hirsch
MAUDE LOCKETT Susan Penhaligon
PENNY SEWELL Lucy Jenkins
SIMON ST CLAIR Patrick Pearson
Voice of HENRY LOCKETT Timothy West

AUTHOR'S NOTE
It would be embarrassing to list all the people who read the script of this play at various stages of its evolution, and made valuable comments and suggestions for its improvement, but I should like to acknowledge the assistance and encouragement of three persons in particular: Patrick Garland, Mike Ockrent and John Adams.

                                    DL

DRAMATIS PERSONAE
(*in order of appearance*)

JEREMY DEANE
LEO RAFKIN
MAUDE LOCKETT
PENNY SEWELL
SIMON ST CLAIR
Also: Voice of HENRY LOCKETT

The action takes place at the Wheatcroft
Centre, a seventeenth-century farmhouse
and barn in Dorset, converted to
accommodate short residential courses in
creative writing. The time is a recent
summer.

ACT ONE

Act One Scene One. Early afternoon.

A converted seventeenth-century barn. An open-plan sitting-room, with door stage left giving direct access to the outside, and two interior doors leading to a bedroom and a bathroom on the ground floor. An open (preferably spiral) staircase leads to a gallery landing, with a door leading to a second bedroom. The bedrooms, insofar as their interiors are visible, are austerely furnished with single beds, upright chairs, chests of drawers, pegs on walls. The sitting room is furnished with well-worn, non-matching furniture: a sofa, an armchair, and a coffee table centre stage; a trestle table that serves as a desk, with a battered swivel-chair, and a couple of wooden folding chairs, stage right. Downstage left there is a small L-shaped sink unit and work-surface, with electric kettle, instant coffee and teabags on it, and storage for cups, glasses, etc., underneath, and a high stool beside it. Downstage right is an answerphone, with monitor facility and volume control, on a small table with drawer. Rush matting on the stone floor. A small bookshelf mounted on the wall near the downstairs bedroom door contains some well-worn reference books, dictionaries, etc., and a random selection of literary paperbacks. The general effect should be rustic, improvised, and not particularly comfortable. Mounted on the rear wall stage left there is a bust of a distinguished-looking elderly man made some time in the last thirty years.
The outside door opens.

> JEREMY (*off*)
> Here we are.

JEREMY, wearing cardigan and corduroy trousers, comes in, carrying a suitcase, followed by LEO, in sports jacket and lightweight trousers, carrying a portable computer in a case. JEREMY is a middle-aged bachelor, slightly fussy in manner. LEO is about fifty, American-Jewish, quite handsome in a grizzled, furrowed way. He looks somewhat depressed and apprehensive.

JEREMY

It's a converted barn, as you can see. (*He puts down the suitcase*) There are two bedrooms, one up, one down. (*He points*) Bathroom and loo in here. (*He indicates the second door on the ground floor*) Maude hasn't arrived yet, so you can take your pick of the bedrooms.

LEO

Which one do you recommend?

JEREMY

Well, some people in the upstairs room do complain of the birds in the eaves.

LEO

I'll take the downstairs one. (*He puts the computer on the coffee table, and picks up suitcase*) It's a pretty old building, isn't it?

JEREMY

Seventeenth-century. Like the farmhouse.

LEO

Stone floors. Must be cold as hell in the winter.

LEO *carries his case into the ground-floor bedroom.* JEREMY *follows him to the door, and leans against the door frame.*

JEREMY

Ah, we close from December to March.

LEO *throws case onto bed, opens it and unpacks a few items.*

LEO (*projects voice*)

So what do you do then, Jeremy?

JEREMY

I usually go to Morocco. I sit in the sun and write poetry.

LEO

You're a poet, huh? As well as running this place?

JEREMY

Well, I have published a slim volume or two . . . I could show you some of my work if you're interested.

JEREMY *takes a slim volume from the bookshelf.*

> **LEO**
> I don't know anything about poetry. I don't really
> understand why people go on writing the stuff.
> Nobody reads it anymore, except other poets. (*Comes
> to doorway*) I don't mean to be personal.

JEREMY *conceals his book behind his back.*

> **JEREMY**
> Oh, point taken! The audience is minuscule. But I
> suppose one goes on because one is obsessed with the
> *music* of language.

> **LEO**
> Music?

> **JEREMY**
> Sounds, rhythms, cadences.

> **LEO**
> Well, you can get those things into prose.

> **JEREMY**
> Oh yes, I agree, absolutely. Your short stories –
> they're just like poems, I always think.

> **LEO**
> I hope not.

> **JEREMY**
> I mean –

> **LEO** (*smiles faintly*)
> Sure, I know what you mean, Jeremy.

LEO *comes out into the sitting-room.* JEREMY *covertly replaces his book on the bookshelf.*

> **LEO**
> We share this room – Maude Lockett and I?

> **JEREMY**
> Yes, it's a place where you can read the students'
> work, or see them individually. (*Smiles*) Or just get
> away from them for a bit.

3

Act One Scene One

LEO *looks slightly anxious.*

> LEO
> How many are there in this course?

> JEREMY
> Sixteen.

> LEO
> Is that all?

> JEREMY
> Twenty is our maximum, and I'm afraid a few
> cancelled when Maurice Denton had to withdraw. He
> has rather a following here. It was ever so good of you
> to step in at such short notice.

> LEO
> How did you know I was in England?

> JEREMY
> There was an interview in the *Guardian*, a few weeks
> ago.

> LEO
> Oh yeah.

> JEREMY
> It mentioned that you taught creative writing at the
> University of Illinois. I thought you might find it
> interesting to compare British students.

> LEO (*doubtfully*)
> If they're all fans of Maurice Denton . . . I tried one of
> his books. Never finished it.

> JEREMY
> Oh, I'm sure you'll have them eating out of your hand
> in no time.

> LEO
> Where do *I* eat, since we're on the subject?

> JEREMY
> In the main house. You forage for breakfast and
> lunch. The students take turns to prepare the evening

meal, and wash up afterwards. You and Maude don't have to, of course.

LEO

I'm glad to hear it.

JEREMY

Though some tutors muck in and the students rather like it if they do.

A pause. LEO *does not rise to the hint.* JEREMY *goes over to the sink.*

JEREMY

You can make yourself a cup of tea or coffee here. (*He pulls the plug out of the sink and peers in*) Oh Gawd!

LEO

What's the matter?

JEREMY

Last week's community playwrights seem to have clogged up the sink with their Lapsang Suchong. I *told* them to use teabags.

LEO

D'you have a, whaddyacallit, plumber's helper?

JEREMY

I think we call it a plumber's mate. There's one over in the farmhouse. (*Pokes sink outlet*) Ugh. I suppose one could call this a particularly unpleasant form of writer's block.

JEREMY *chuckles at his own joke, but* LEO *seems to think that writer's block is no laughing matter.*

JEREMY

Would you like a cup of tea?

LEO

I could use a cup of coffee.

JEREMY

It's only instant, I'm afraid.

Act One Scene One

JEREMY *fills the kettle and switches it on.* LEO *begins unpacking the word processor.*

> **JEREMY**
>
> I see you've brought your typewriter with you.
>
> **LEO**
>
> It's not a typewriter, it's a portable word processor. Where can I plug it in?
>
> **JEREMY**
>
> There's a socket over there. I may have to get you an adaptor. It's a rather eccentric wiring system, with a special sort of plug that you can't buy any more . . . Were you hoping to do some writing yourself, then?
>
> **LEO**
>
> You mean I won't have time?
>
> **JEREMY**
>
> Well the students *will* bring their unpublished novels with them, though we tell them not to, and expect the tutors to read them. (LEO *looks unhappy*) You just have to be firm.
>
> **LEO**
>
> Firm?
>
> **JEREMY**
>
> Ration them. Only one *magnum opus* per person.
>
> **LEO**
>
> I'm beginning to think this was a very bad idea.
>
> **JEREMY** (*cheerfully*)
>
> Oh, you'll love it! Everybody does, in the end. There's such an *atmosphere* at the end of a successful course.
>
> **LEO**
>
> What about unsuccessful courses? Do they have an atmosphere too?
>
> **JEREMY**
>
> A course taught by Leo Rafkin and Maude Lockett *has* to be a success . . . Have you met her?

LEO

No.

JEREMY

She's charming. No side at all. Have you read her
novels?

LEO

One or two.

JEREMY

To tell you the truth, I don't care awfully for them,
myself. I can take just so much about periods and
miscarriages and breast-feeding and so on.

LEO

I know what you mean.

JEREMY

After a while it gets on my tits . . . But she's awfully
nice. Awfully good with the students.

LEO

Is she married?

JEREMY

Very much so. To an Oxford don. They have four
children, I believe. And you?

LEO

I have three children by two wives, to neither of whom
I am married at the moment.

JEREMY

Ah.

JEREMY *goes over to the sink unit. He lays his hand on the side of
the kettle.*

JEREMY

If the kettle doesn't seem to be warming up, give it a
bang like this. (*He gives the kettle a blow.*)

LEO

You don't seem to be into hi-tech here.

JEREMY

No. But we do have an answerphone. (*He goes over to the telephone to point it out.*)

LEO (*ironically*)

Terrific.

JEREMY

The tutors were always complaining because they couldn't telephone from here, and then, when we had one put in last year, they complained because they kept getting interrupted. So we bought an answerphone. It's brand new.

LEO

The students – who are they?

JEREMY

Oh, all kinds. Housewives, retired people, unemployed.

LEO

How do you select them?

JEREMY

Oh, we don't *select* them. They just apply. First come, first served.

LEO

So how do you know they can write?

JEREMY

Well, we don't. (LEO *looks dismayed*) That's what makes the Wheatcroft such fun.

LEO

Fun?

JEREMY

It's so unpredictable.

The kettle boils. JEREMY *spoons coffee and pours water into two cups.*

JEREMY

Milk and sugar? Sterilised milk, I'm afraid.

LEO
No, just black.

LEO *takes the coffee from* JEREMY.

LEO
Why Wheatcroft?

JEREMY *gestures towards the bust.*

JEREMY
After our founder. Aubrey Wheatcroft.

LEO
Who was he?

JEREMY
A rather idealistic minor poet with a private income.
He left all his money to endow this place. He believed
that there are untapped reserves of creativity in
everyone, which can be released in the right
environment.

LEO
You mean, like stone floors and birds in the eaves?

JEREMY
Well, yes, he did specify a rural setting. But the social
situation is more important. Bringing together people
who want to be writers with people who *are* writers, in
an isolated farmhouse, for four or five days. Having
them eat together, work together, relax together.
Readings, workshops, tutorials, informal discussions.
It *has* to have a stimulating effect. It's like a pressure
cooker.

A pause, while LEO *ponders this metaphor. He puts down his coffee.*

LEO
I'm leaving.

LEO *goes back into the bedroom, and begins hastily repacking his
case.* JEREMY *follows him to the bedroom door.*

JEREMY (*aghast*)
Leaving? But why? You can't.

> LEO
> I'm sorry. I should never have agreed to come here.

> JEREMY
> But what have I said?

> LEO
> Nothing but the truth, Jeremy.

> JEREMY
> I don't understand.

LEO *brings his suitcase out of the bedroom and puts his computer back into its case.*

> LEO
> I got the wrong idea. I thought I would be giving a few regular classes to regular students, and otherwise be free to get on with my own work. I didn't know it was going to be . . . a pressure cooker.

> JEREMY
> But what about the students? They've paid money.

> LEO
> Not for me. For Maurice Denton. Or Maude Lockett.

> JEREMY
> You can't ask Maude to do the whole thing on her own.

LEO *has both cases in his hands, ready to go.*

> LEO
> Oh, I'm sure she can handle it. A woman who has brought up four children, writes a weekly book review in *The Times*, seems to be on TV or radio every other day, and has published ten bestselling novels –

During this speech, MAUDE *appears at the door, suitcase in hand. She is a good-looking, confident woman in her forties, dressed casually but expensively.*

> MAUDE
> Nine, actually.

JEREMY (*turns*)
Maude! (*He hastens forward to greet her*) I didn't hear
your car. (*He takes her hand and kisses her on the cheek.*)

MAUDE
Jeremy, how nice to see you. (*Advances towards* LEO
and extends her hand) And you must be Leo Rafkin.

LEO (*shaking her hand*)
Hallo.

MAUDE
It's nine novels, actually, and number nine was
published rather longer ago than I like to think about,
no doubt because of all those book reviews and TV
shows.

LEO (*embarrassed*)
I'm sorry. I, um, I didn't mean . . .

MAUDE (*smiling*)
It doesn't matter.

JEREMY
Maude, Leo says he's leaving. Do persuade him to
stay.

MAUDE *looks enquiringly at* LEO, *who is already beginning to
change his mind.*

LEO
Well, the more Jeremy told me about the course . . .

MAUDE
Goodness, Jeremy, whatever did you tell him?

LEO
He said it was a pressure cooker.

JEREMY
That was just a metaphor, for heaven's sake!

LEO
It sounds too intimate. A class is a class as far as I'm
concerned, not an encounter group.

JEREMY (*plaintively*)
You don't *have* to be chummy with the students. As
long as you comment on their work.

MAUDE
That's right. It might make us a rather effective team.
You could be very mean and hard on them, and then I
could come along and be constructive and
sympathetic. Isn't that how interrogators work?

LEO *looks uncertain whether she is mocking him or not.*

JEREMY
Oh, do please stay. Everybody will be so disappointed
if you don't.

MAUDE
There's no point forcing Mr Rafkin, Jeremy. If he
doesn't feel up to it . . .

LEO (*bridling*)
It's not a question of being 'up to it'.

JEREMY
Give it a trial, at least. One day.

Pause. LEO *glances at* MAUDE, *hoping she will second this appeal.*
She is silent.

LEO
Well, all right.

JEREMY
Oh, super.

MAUDE
That's settled, then. Where am I sleeping?

LEO (*quickly*)
I took the downstairs bedroom.

MAUDE
Oh, how kind of you.

LEO (*disconcerted*)
Kind?

MAUDE
Yes, it's rather damp, haven't you noticed? And you get a lot of beetles in there.

LEO *gives a sickly smile.*

JEREMY
Let me take your bag upstairs, Maude.

MAUDE
Thanks, Jeremy.

JEREMY *takes* MAUDE'S *case up the staircase and into the upper bedroom.*

LEO
You've obviously been here before.

MAUDE
Many times. I'm dying for a cup of tea. What about you?

LEO
No thanks.

MAUDE *goes to sink unit, and, during the ensuing dialogue, makes herself a cup of tea with a tea-bag. She shows her familiarity with the place by slapping the kettle.*

MAUDE (*looks into sink*)
Oh dear, something seems to be blocking the sink.

LEO
Community playwrights.

MAUDE
Really?

LEO
You must like coming here.

MAUDE
Yes, I do.

LEO
I mean, you can hardly need the money.

MAUDE (*registering the statement as slightly impertinent*)

No, I hardly can. But then I don't suppose you came for the sake of a fee, either, Mr Rafkin.

LEO

Please call me Leo. It was an impulse. My work wasn't going too well. I thought a change of scene might help.

JEREMY *comes quietly out of the bedroom and stands on the landing, unwilling to interrupt.*

LEO

As you probably know, I'm spending six months in England, working on a book.

MAUDE

No, I didn't know.

LEO

It was in the *Guardian*.

MAUDE

Ah. We take *The Times* and the *Independent*.

LEO

I'm on leave from my University. I have a Guggenheim.

MAUDE (*hint of mockery*)

Congratulations.

LEO

I'm writing a novel about the end of World War Two in Europe.

MAUDE

Ambitious.

LEO

It is.

JEREMY

Er, I'd better get back to the farmhouse or the students will be feeling all neglected. Is there anything we should discuss about the course?

MAUDE
I thought we'd stick to the usual pattern.

JEREMY
It seems to work best.

LEO
What is the usual pattern?

JEREMY (*with the air of someone repeating a set speech*)
This evening, after dinner, is for everybody to get to know each other. Tomorrow morning you two should explain how you're going to organise the course. We think it's a good idea if they write something new while they're here, not just revise the stuff they've brought with them.

LEO (*ironically*)
You mean, like write a novel in four days.

JEREMY
Well, it has been known, believe it or not. But no, something like a chapter, or a short story.

LEO
Somebody wrote an entire novel in four days?

JEREMY
Yes, he sat up every night, on benzedrine or something.

MAUDE
Was the novel any good?

JEREMY
It was before my time. I shouldn't think so.

LEO
Still, to create an entire world in four days. Even God took six. I'd like to meet that guy.

JEREMY
Anyway, on Day One, after the plenary, you and Maude should see the students individually. Some may need encouragement to start writing.

LEO
To start?

JEREMY
Yes.

LEO
You mean, some of these people have never written
anything before?

JEREMY
Obviously they have a feeling that they'd *like* to write.

LEO *shakes his head disbelievingly.*

LEO (*sotto voce*)
Jesus Christ.

JEREMY
Tomorrow evening, either you or Maude will read
from your work, and then the other one will read on
the following evening. You did bring something,
didn't you?

LEO
Yeah.

MAUDE
Your novel about the War?

LEO
I never read from work in progress.

MAUDE
Why?

LEO
If the audience doesn't give you ten minutes' standing
ovation at the end, you lose faith in it.

MAUDE
Oh, I'm just the opposite. I like to try things out.

JEREMY
On the third evening, we have the visiting writer.

LEO
Another writer?

JEREMY

Yes, we've found that at this point in the course, when everybody knows everybody else pretty well, and the atmosphere may be getting a little too cosy, it's good to introduce a catalyst. Someone with a completely different perspective. He, or she, comes for just one night – gives a reading after dinner and goes off next morning.

LEO

Who's coming?

JEREMY

Simon St Clair.

LEO

That asshole?

JEREMY (*with an alarmed glance at* MAUDE)

You know him?

LEO

He interviewed me once, in Chicago. Flattered the hell out of me, then went away and wrote a lot of sneers and smears.

JEREMY

Oh. I didn't know that of course when I . . .

MAUDE

I don't suppose he meant any real harm, Leo.

LEO

Oh yes he did, harm is exactly what he meant. Have you met this guy?

MAUDE

Occasionally.

JEREMY

He won't be here for long, anyway. The next day is the last one. Final efforts by the students, then an early dinner and afterwards *they* read from *their* work. It's a kind of *rite de passage*. It usually turns into a party with everybody getting rather tired and emotional. The course disperses next morning, after breakfast.

> LEO
>
> Well, that's something to look forward to.

> MAUDE
>
> Oh, don't be such a misery!

> LEO (*startled*)
>
> What?

> MAUDE
>
> If you want to go, for God's sake go! I'd rather teach the whole course myself, than have you moaning and whingeing for the next four days.

A pause.

> LEO
>
> I said I'll stay, and I'll stay.

LEO *stalks into his bedroom and shuts the door.* MAUDE *looks at* JEREMY *and makes a grimace, half-amused, half-exasperated.*

> JEREMY
>
> Well, I'd better be running along. (*Sotto voce*) It's a bit awkward, him having a grudge against Simon.

> MAUDE
>
> Mmm. It's a pity Simon isn't the other tutor.

> JEREMY
>
> I did ask him.

> MAUDE (*with affected casualness*)
>
> Did you tell him I suggested it?

> JEREMY
>
> No, I wasn't sure if you . . . Should I have done?

> MAUDE
>
> No. I don't know. It's of no importance now, anyway.

> JEREMY
>
> He said he's taken a vow never to teach a Wheatcroft course again.

MAUDE
Why?

JEREMY
Last time a Jehovah's Witness tried to convert him
and a policeman got drunk and threw up all over his
designer jeans.

MAUDE
How very unlucky.

JEREMY
Well, he did provoke them rather . . . I think he only
agreed to come back as visiting writer because you
were going to be here.

The telephone rings twice then stops.

MAUDE (*surprised*)
Is there a telephone in here?

JEREMY
Yes, an answerphone. It rings twice and then starts
recording. It's one of those sneaky ones where you can
listen in to the other person leaving their message.

The amplified voice of HENRY LOCKETT (*a middle-aged Oxford
don*) *is heard from the answerphone. The actors on stage speak over
his monologue.*

HENRY'S VOICE
**Oh, hallo, er, this is Henry Lockett for Maude
Lockett . . .**

MAUDE
Henry!

HENRY'S VOICE
**Er, Maude, I've lost my, that is to say I can't seem
to find my cufflinks, I mean I can't find a pair that
match, and, er, there's a College Feast tonight and,
er, I should feel rather a prat with odd cufflinks . . .**

JEREMY
You can pick it up and speak to him, you know.

MAUDE

No, I don't want to. I think this a retrograde step, Jeremy, I come here to get away from domestic concerns.

HENRY'S VOICE

. . . I was wondering whether you've seen any of them anywhere, the missing ones, that is, and picked them up . . .

MAUDE

How did he know the number, anyway?

JEREMY

I suppose he phoned the farmhouse, and someone over there gave it to him.

HENRY'S VOICE

. . . or did Mrs Grimshaw perhaps, when she was doing our bedroom, you don't think, I mean is it possible that she sucked them up in the vacuum cleaner, God I hope not, do you think I should go through the dust bag and if not where the hell are they . . .?

MAUDE

Can't we turn him off?

JEREMY

I think there's a volume control on it somewhere. I'm not very good at these gadgets.

JEREMY *goes over to the phone and peers helplessly at it. He has an inspiration, opens the drawer in the table, and takes out an instruction booklet. He consults this, frowning.*

JEREMY

God! It's all in Arabic . . . Ah, here we are.

JEREMY *rotates the page, trying to make sense of a diagram.*

HENRY'S VOICE

. . . I looked in your jewellery box but they, that is the red velvet one – have you got another? Anyway, they aren't, I thought you might have put them in there, but they aren't there . . .

LEO *opens the door of his bedroom and looks out with a puzzled expression.*

> MAUDE (*to* LEO)
> My husband. (*To* JEREMY) For God's sake pull the plug out, Jeremy!

LEO *goes across to phone.*

> HENRY'S VOICE
> . . . Anyway, if you've any idea where any of my cufflinks are please, other than the odd ones I've got of course, please phone me back as soon as possible. Oh, and by the way, I've accepted the invitation to that conference –

LEO *turns down volume, silencing phone.*

> MAUDE
> Thank you.

> LEO
> You're welcome.

JEREMY *looks from one to the other.*

> JEREMY
> Well, see you both at dinner.

Blackout.

Act One Scene Two. Later the same evening.

The barn. The sitting-room is empty and dark.

> MAUDE (*voice off*)
> Goodnight, Jeremy! See you in the morning.

Sounds of LEO *and* MAUDE *approaching from outside. The door opens, and* MAUDE *fumbles for the lightswitch. The light comes on.* MAUDE *enters, followed by* LEO, *who is holding a plumber's mate.*

> MAUDE
> There! That wasn't so bad, was it?

Act One Scene Two

    LEO

You make it sound like I'd just been to the dentist.

    MAUDE

Well, you had the waiting-room look, exactly, just before dinner. Are you going to have a go at the sink?

LEO *puts the plumber's mate down on the sink-unit.*

    LEO

Tomorrow. How about a nightcap? I have a bottle of scotch in my bag.

    MAUDE (*slight hesitation*)

Well . . . All right. That would be nice.

MAUDE *sits down on the sofa.* LEO *goes into his bedroom, leaving the door open, to fetch the bottle of scotch.* MAUDE *projects her voice.*

    MAUDE

Who was the grey-haired lady you were sitting next to at dinner?

    LEO

A retired schoolteacher. I didn't catch her name.

    MAUDE

You seemed to be very deep in conversation.

    LEO (*emerging from bedroom with bottle*)

It dawned on me after about ten minutes that she thinks I wrote *The Catcher in the Rye*. I didn't have the heart to disillusion her.

    MAUDE (*laughs*)

And what did you make of Penny?

    LEO

Penny?

    MAUDE

Mrs Sewell, from South Wales. Big eyes and fair hair.

LEO *goes to sink unit and pours two glasses of scotch.*

    LEO

I didn't get much out of her.

MAUDE

I thought she was very nice.

LEO

Water? There doesn't seem to be any ice.

MAUDE

Please.

LEO *adds a little water to* MAUDE*'s glass and takes the two glasses over to the sofa.*

LEO

They're all *nice* enough. The question is, can they write?

MAUDE

Well, we shall see. These courses *are* a bit of a leap in the dark.

LEO (*raises glass*)

Geronimo.

MAUDE

Hmm?

LEO

It's what paratroopers say as they jump out the plane. (*He drinks.*)

MAUDE (*smiles, drinks*)

Geronimo, then. I'm glad you decided to stay. I've admired your work for ages.

LEO

Including *Wise Virgins and Other Stories*?

MAUDE (*evasively*)

That was your first book, wasn't it?

LEO

You didn't like it so much when you reviewed it for the *Spectator*.

MAUDE

Oh, that was a very long time ago. I'm surprised you remember it.

LEO

I remember all my reviews.

MAUDE

Goodness, I hardly bother to read mine.

LEO

I never believe writers who say that.

MAUDE *looks as if she is going to take offence, but backs off.*

MAUDE

Well, Henry reads them for me. He only shows me the nice ones.

LEO

My wife – my last wife – only showed me the bad ones. She used to go to the library and photocopy them specially. That's how I saw your review.

MAUDE (*laughs uncertainly*)

I can't imagine I said anything really nasty about *The Wise Virgin*.

LEO

Wise Virgins. You said, 'Mr Rafkin polishes his style, the better to see in it the reflection of his own ego.'

MAUDE

Did I? You know, you really shouldn't attach so much importance to what critics say.

LEO

That's easy for you to say. You're a best-seller.

MAUDE

Well, not in the Jackie Collins class . . . if class is the word I want.

LEO

But whether you get good reviews or bad reviews, you're sure to sell twenty thousand in hardback, eighty thousand in paperback – right?

MAUDE

Yes, I suppose so. You seem remarkably well informed about my sales.

LEO

There was an article in the *Bookseller* recently, by your publisher. I'm not that kind of writer. My books are literature. I don't mean yours aren't literature too –

MAUDE (*ironically*)

Oh, thanks.

LEO

But yours sell at Heathrow as well as Hatchards. Mine don't. They earn me more money indirectly than directly. They win prizes, they attract grants, they justify my salary as a college teacher. So you see I'm highly sensitive to criticism. Favourable reviews are *currency* to me.

MAUDE (*with exaggerated contrition*)

I'm sorry I was unkind about *Wise Virgins*.

LEO

Oh, don't let it worry you. I never did have any luck in England. (*He picks up* MAUDE'S *glass*) Let me freshen your drink.

MAUDE

No more, thanks.

LEO *ignores this refusal, and refills her glass and his own at the sink unit.*

LEO

Tell me about Henry.

MAUDE (*slightly startled*)

Henry? What about him?

LEO

He's a college teacher, isn't he?

MAUDE

He's Reader in the History of Philosophy at Oxford, actually.

LEO *gives drink to* MAUDE. *She puts it down on the coffee table without tasting it.* LEO *sits down beside her on the sofa.*

LEO

He doesn't mind you teaching this course?

MAUDE

No. Why should he mind?

LEO

If I were married to a woman as attractive as you, I wouldn't want her to go away for nearly a week on her own.

MAUDE (*smiles*)

Oh, Henry isn't jealous.

LEO

I don't mean jealous. I mean, if I was married to a woman as attractive as you, I'd want to make love at least every other night.

MAUDE *is surprised, but not flustered, by this pass.*

MAUDE

Oh, I see. Well, after twenty years, you know, desire can be contained for a week or so without too much difficulty. (*She picks up glass and drinks.*)

LEO

Twenty years! You've been married to the same guy for twenty years?

MAUDE

I'm afraid so. (*She glances at her watch*) I think it's time I went to bed. I'm feeling rather tired from the drive down. (*She stands up.*)

LEO (*getting up*)

Oh, have another.

MAUDE

No, thank you. Shall I use the bathroom first?

LEO

Sure. Go ahead.

MAUDE

Goodnight, then. See you in the morning.

LEO
Goodnight.

MAUDE *ascends the stairs, watched by* LEO, *and goes into her bedroom.* LEO *swallows the last of his drink, takes the two glasses over to the sink and rinses them. He seems restless and uncertain what to do. He examines the bust of Aubrey Wheatcroft perfunctorily; he takes down and leafs through* JEREMY's *book of poems without reading it. Upstairs,* MAUDE *takes off her dress and puts a dressing-gown over her slip. She exchanges her shoes for slippers. Carrying a sponge bag, she comes out of the room. As* MAUDE *descends the stairs,* LEO *goes into his bedroom and closes the door.* MAUDE *goes into the bathroom and closes the door.* LEO *opens the door of his room, and lurks just inside the threshold. Sound of toilet flushing.* LEO, *not wishing to ambush* MAUDE *too obviously, goes into sitting-room, moves towards the table, changes his mind and rapidly crosses the room to the sink. He picks up plumber's mate and goes through motions of unblocking the sink, glancing occasionally at bathroom door. The bathroom door opens and* MAUDE *comes out. She sees* LEO *and smiles politely.*

MAUDE
It's all yours.

LEO
Thanks. I'm not making much progress with this sink.

MAUDE
Leave it to Jeremy.

MAUDE *begins to ascend the stairs.*

LEO
You were right about my room being damp.

MAUDE
Oh, it shouldn't be too bad at this time of year.

LEO
And those bugs you mentioned – I have a phobia about creepy-crawlies. I don't think I'm going to sleep well in there.

MAUDE *stops on staircase.*

MAUDE (*with a sigh of impatience*)
You mean you want to exchange rooms?

LEO
No. (*Beat*) I thought I might share yours.

MAUDE
Oh, I don't think that would be a good idea.

LEO
Why not?

MAUDE
Well, for one thing, there's only a single bed, and it's extremely narrow.

LEO
I could bring my mattress up. We could put the two mattresses on the floor.

MAUDE (*laughs, a little forced*)
You really have the most extraordinary cheek. What makes you think that I would want to sleep with you?

LEO
It might make a change from Henry.

MAUDE *begins to climb the stairs again.*

LEO
Maude! Sorry – I shouldn't have said that.

LEO, *still holding the plumber's mate, moves forward to stand beneath the gallery landing, where* MAUDE *stops and looks down at him. They are in a Romeo and Juliet posture.*

MAUDE
I think we'd better get some things straight.

LEO
Sure. You mean safe sex? Don't worry – I'll take care of it.

MAUDE
I mean I don't find you irresistibly attractive, and I'm not in the habit of sleeping with complete strangers.

LEO

I'm not a complete stranger. You've read my work.

MAUDE

And didn't much like it, as you just reminded me.

LEO

You've read my work, I've read yours. We already
know more about each other than many lovers of long
standing.

MAUDE

I don't know about your books, but mine are works of
fiction.

LEO

Ah, yes, fiction. Come on, Maude, you know that
everything you write comes out of yourself, ultimately.
If it isn't your experience speaking, it's your
unconscious.

MAUDE

This is all very interesting, but why don't you save it
for the students?

LEO

I'll level with you, Maude. I didn't come here because
I wanted a change, or because I wanted to check out
British creative-writing students. I came to meet you.

MAUDE

Oh? Why?

LEO

You intrigued me. That photograph on your dust
jackets – with the Mona Lisa smile. The amazing
number of books you've written. The sales figures in
the *Bookseller*. Beauty, fertility, and money. An
irresistible combination.

MAUDE

The resistance seems to be all on my side. Goodnight.
(*She moves towards the bedroom door.*)

LEO

And then I read the books.

MAUDE *stops, turns.*

> MAUDE
> I do hope you're not going to pay me any insincere compliments.

> LEO
> Your heroines are all sleeping beauties, aren't they? Passionate but unfulfilled women, half-longing, half-fearing to be awakened.

> MAUDE
> And you thought you would play Prince Charming?

> LEO
> We could play Beauty and the Beast if you prefer.

> MAUDE
> Goodnight.

MAUDE *goes into the bedroom, closes the door and locks it, leaving* LEO *staring impotently at it. He relieves his feelings by planting the plumber's mate on the head of Aubrey Wheatcroft.*

Blackout.

Act One Scene Three.
Late afternoon of the following day.

The barn. LEO *is alone, typing on his word processor at the trestle table. At one end of the table is a pile of manuscripts in folders. There is a tentative knock at the door.* LEO, *displeased at the interruption, does not look up or round.*

> LEO
> Yeah.

Another knock.

> LEO (*louder*)
> Come in!

The door opens and PENNY *enters. She is a young woman, who might be in her late twenties or early thirties. She has big eyes and*

30

long fair hair. She wears a simple summer dress and carries a floppy
sunhat. She has a transparent sincerity of manner which sometimes
seems like naivety, and speaks with a perceptible Welsh accent.
(NOTE: *She could have any kind of looks, providing they contrast*
with Maude's, and any provincial accent. MAUDE'*s description of*
her at the beginning of Act One Scene Two, p. 22, should be
adjusted accordingly.)

> PENNY (*looking round*)
> Excuse me, I was looking for Maude Lockett.
>
> LEO
> She's gone for a walk.
>
> PENNY
> Oh.
>
> LEO
> Down by the river, I think.
>
> PENNY
> Oh, I see. (*Hesitantly*) I was wondering whether she'd
> had a chance to look at the chapter I left this morning.
>
> LEO
> We shared the stuff between us. What was yours
> called?
>
> PENNY
> *Lights and Shadows.* That's the provisional title of the
> novel.
>
> LEO (*frowns*)
> I think I read that one.

LEO *reaches for the pile of manuscripts, and sifts through them. He*
pulls out one.

> LEO
> You're Penny Sewell, right?
>
> PENNY
> Yes.
>
> LEO
> Yeah. The privilege fell to me. *Lights and Shadows.*

Act One Scene Three

LEO *leafs through the manuscript.*

> PENNY
>
> What do you think of that as a title? Or perhaps you
> don't think titles are important?

> LEO
>
> Oh, I think they're very important – to the writer. I
> always tell my students back home, the title should
> remind you what your story is supposed to be *about*.

> PENNY
>
> Well, *Lights and Shadows* does that for me, I think.

> LEO
>
> Yeah, it's OK. It's about the best thing in here. After
> the title there's a steady decline.

> PENNY (*crestfallen*)
>
> You don't like it?

> LEO
>
> Did you expect me to?

> PENNY
>
> I didn't know what to expect. I've never shown my
> work to anyone before. What's wrong with it?

> LEO
>
> Well, it isn't very interesting, and the style is
> derivative.

> PENNY
>
> Derivative?

> LEO
>
> From Virginia Woolf, chiefly.

> PENNY (*submissively*)
>
> Yes, I do like Virginia Woolf.

> LEO (*reads*)
>
> 'Was this all there was, then, all there was to life, her
> life anyway, she thought, peeling the potatoes at the
> sink, and looking out through the kitchen window at
> the small square of lawn, where the toys abandoned by
> Ben and Jessica lay scattered like the remnants of some

horrible accident, a car crash or an air crash, touched poignantly by the golden beams of the sun that was setting like an inflamed eye behind the red roofs of the neighbouring houses.' (*Looks up*) If the sun is inflamed, which means red, would the sunbeams be golden?

PENNY

No, of course not. How stupid of me.

LEO

It comes from over-using the pathetic fallacy.

PENNY

What's that?

LEO

Making the external world reflect metaphorically the emotions of the perceiver.

PENNY

Oh.

LEO

Like 'touched poignantly' and 'inflamed eye'.

PENNY

But apart from that . . .

LEO

There isn't much apart from that, is there? The whole chapter is saturated in the pathetic fallacy.

PENNY

You don't think I should persevere with it?

LEO

I don't see that it's likely to get any better. Do you?

LEO *holds out the manuscript. Pause.*

PENNY (*quietly*)

No, I'm sure you're right.

PENNY *takes her manuscript from* LEO *and almost runs out of the barn. The door slams shut behind her.* LEO *rises from the table and moves towards the door as if to call her back. But then he stops, shrugs and returns to the table. He settles himself to work again. He*

begins to type. The outside door opens and MAUDE *enters, rather*
aggressively.

> MAUDE
> Penny Sewell seems to be upset. She ran straight past
> me.

LEO *continues to type.*

> MAUDE
> Was that your doing?

LEO *sighs and pushes back his chair.*

> LEO
> She asked me a straight question and I gave her a
> straight answer.

> MAUDE
> What was the question?

> LEO
> She asked me if she should go on with her novel.

> MAUDE
> And you said 'No.'

Pause.

> My God, I can hardly believe it. And you call yourself
> a teacher?

> LEO
> With more right than you, I believe.

> MAUDE
> A teacher is supposed to encourage, isn't he? To make
> the most of people's potential?

> LEO
> A teacher is supposed to tell the truth, whether it's
> welcome or not.

> MAUDE
> Even if it means strangling talent at birth?

> LEO
> I want to strangle no-talent at birth. It's merciful in
> the long run.

MAUDE

How can you be so sure that she has no talent.

LEO

Nobody on this course has any talent. (*He thumps the pile of manuscripts*) They're all a bunch of amateurs. They're the literary equivalent of Sunday painters.

MAUDE

What's wrong with that? If they get some satisfaction out of expressing themselves in words . . .

LEO

Writing is not just self-expression. It's communication.

MAUDE

But that's precisely what this place is for! To give people an audience – a critical, but sympathetic and supportive audience. People who've been writing in complete isolation, for years perhaps, hiding their novel in a drawer, afraid to show it to their husband or their wife, or to friends, for fear of being laughed at, misunderstood. They come here to be *read*.

LEO

This isn't real reading, what goes on here.

MAUDE

What d'you mean?

LEO

It's reading under duress. The students know that. What they really want to learn from us is, how to get published. But they haven't a snowball's chance in hell of getting this stuff into print (*he indicates the manuscripts*), and they might as well be told now.

MAUDE

I don't agree.

LEO

Otherwise little Mrs Penny Sewell, as well as all the other frustrations and disappointments of her life, which, I infer from her novel, include a career

35

prematurely terminated by marriage, a husband who
doesn't appreciate her, a mother-in-law who spoils her
two children, and a loathing for the pattern of the
bedroom wallpaper which she chose in a rash moment
because the one she really wanted was too expensive –
on top of all that she's going to have to cope with a
steady stream of rejected manuscripts in self-addressed
envelopes falling on to the doormat every morning for
the rest of her life.

MAUDE

Well, that's her choice. You shouldn't presume to
make it for her.

Pause.

LEO

Have you talked to Brigstock?

MAUDE

Brigstock?

LEO

The military-looking guy, with the moustache.

MAUDE

Oh, Lionel. What about him?

LEO

Did you know that he has written twelve unpublished
novels?

MAUDE

Really?

LEO

Twelve. Twelve full-length books. Approximately one
million words. All garbage, to judge by this specimen
of number thirteen.

LEO *pulls a thick folder out of the pile of manuscripts and flips over
a page or two.*

MAUDE

I take it he's tried to get them published.

LEO

Has he tried! He told me he's collected two hundred
and thirty-nine rejection slips. He seemed proud of
them in a weird kind of way.

MAUDE (*amused and appalled in spite of herself*)

Poor Lionel! He should be in the *Guinness Book of
Records*.

LEO

It's the only way he'll get into print, believe me. And
d'you know this guy retired early, on a reduced
pension, to write? He sacrificed a perfectly good career
in insurance to this futile ambition, no doubt because
some 'sympathetic and supportive' tutor on a creative
writing course encouraged him.

MAUDE (*bridling*)

Perhaps he's happier writing books, even books
nobody wants to publish, than he would be in some
dreary nine-to-five job. He looks cheerful enough.

LEO

Oh, sure, he looks cheerful. That's what's so pathetic
about him. He's like a guy who's idea of fun is to get
into the ring with a pro boxer and have the shit
knocked out of him. The publishers keep counting
him out, and he keeps getting up off the floor and
coming back for another knockout punch. 'You didn't
like that novel? Never mind, here's another one.' Pow!
(LEO *mimes having his head knocked back by a punch on
the jaw*) He's flat on his ass again. Somebody should
have thrown in the towel for him years ago. You want
to condemn Penny Sewell to that kind of punishment?

MAUDE

You're not trying to tell me, are you, that all your
students in America become successful writers?

LEO

A number of them have had their work published.

MAUDE

But only a minority? A tiny proportion?

LEO

All right, yes. But there's a difference. Several
differences. First, I don't enrol anyone unless they can
show evidence of some talent. Secondly, I warn them
that if they have any ambition to be writers by
profession, they're inviting a long and slow crucifixion.
Years of hard, lonely work. Writing and rewriting and
rewriting again. Getting rejected, getting blocked,
seeing others succeed where you have failed.

MAUDE

My God, I wonder you have any students at all. You
make the whole business sound so grim.

LEO

That's right. I think writing is a grim business.

MAUDE

But it can be such fun, too!

LEO

Fun?

MAUDE

Yes. I don't know anything like the satisfaction that
you get when you find some phrase that you *know* is
right; or some joke that you know will make people
laugh aloud; or some brilliant idea for a twist in the
plot comes to you out of the blue, in mid-sentence,
and you could whoop with delight. And that lovely
feeling as the pages mount up, and you get to that
point when you know you can finish the book, and
finish it well. And when you do finish it, when you
write the last word, you feel quite exhausted, drained,
but deeply contented. There's nothing like that
feeling. Well, there is, actually, one thing.

LEO

Sex?

MAUDE

No, childbirth.

LEO

Ah.

Pause.

The phone rings twice and stops. LEO *and* MAUDE *look towards the phone.*

> MAUDE (*crossly*)
> I bet that's Henry again.

LEO *turns up volume control on answerphone.*

> HENRY'S VOICE
> . . . look, it's a frightful bore but I don't seem to be able to turn off the shower in our bathroom. What's the name of the plumber we use, I mean I know I could just look up somebody in the Yellow Pages but I'd rather have the usual chap because I may have to leave him alone in the house . . .

> LEO
> You want to take it?

> MAUDE
> No.

LEO *turns off sound.* MAUDE *picks up a briefcase and takes a loose-leaf folder out of it.*

> MAUDE
> I need to look over the piece I'm going to read this evening.

> LEO
> I look forward to it.

> MAUDE
> I doubt if it will be your cup of tea

Blackout.

Act One Scene Four. The evening of the same day.

MAUDE *is seated in an upright chair, facing the audience (who thus represent the circle of students listening to her reading). She is lit by a spotlight. The main set is blacked out or curtained off. Beside her is a*

small table with, on it, a glass of water. She has in her hands a
typescript in a loose-leaf folder.

MAUDE

I'd like to read from a novel I started recently. It
seemed to come very easily at first, and then it just
stopped. I've never had that happen to me before. It's
rather disturbing. I thought that if I read it to you this
evening, it might somehow loosen the blockage, get
the gears moving again.

I haven't decided on a title yet, but the heroine is
called Marion Brownlow, a widow of about forty-five,
still quite good-looking, but going through the change
of life, in more ways than one. I might call it *Change of
Life*, as a matter of fact. Her husband died a couple of
years before, and proved to be bankrupt, so Marion is
obliged to live with her daughter, who is married to an
Oxford don, and bullies her. In the second chapter
Marion is invited to dinner by some friends, Vera and
Dennis Moreton. However, what she has really been
invited to is drinks, though she doesn't realise this
until the hostess brings in a tray of dainty canapés and
starts handing round plates and napkins.

MAUDE *drinks from the glass and begins to read.*

By this time Marion had consumed two gin-and-tonics
and three glasses of Entre-Deux-Mers on an empty
stomach. She had a headache, double vision, and her
intestines were gurgling like old plumbing. She piled
her plate with as many canapés as seemed halfway
decent; but the almost transparent slivers of smoked
salmon on wafer-thin slices of brown bread, the fragile
vol-au-vents that burst like powdery bubbles in the
mouth, the two or three black beads of lumpfish roe
reposing on tiny cushions of cottage cheese, were
hardly sufficient to counteract the effect of the alcohol
she had imbibed, or to satisfy her hunger.

If she had been the only guest she could, of course,
have confessed her error, asked for an omelette, and
they would all have had a good laugh together. But

there were three other people present: Dennis's superior at the Bodley and his wife, and another man whom she hadn't met before, Hamish Sedley, whom she was fairly sure had been invited for her own benefit. He was apparently an old friend who had just come back from a British Council post in South America. He seemed rather nice.

In this carefully assembled and delicately balanced company, Marion dared not admit that she was starving and demand proper sustenance. No, the only thing to do was to refuse any more wine, and hold on tight to the arms of her chair until the coffee appeared. Unfortunately, on top of all her other symptoms, she now felt her entire body break out in perspiration and her cheeks glowing like coals. Vera looked anxiously at her.

'Marion, are you a little too near the fire?' she said. 'Would you like to change places with me?'

'Oh, no!' said Marion, certain that such a manoeuvre was beyond her capability. She added carelessly, 'It's only a hot flush.'

She saw reflected in Vera's face the enormity of her indiscretion; but, dizzy with drink, could feel no shame or regret. 'It's my time of life, I'm afraid,' she said defiantly. Then, with a giggle: 'It's been so cold lately, when I have to walk the dog, I wait till I get a hot flush. It's like portable central heating.'

There was a shocked silence, broken after a few seconds, by a rich, appreciative chuckle. Hamish Sedley –

> JEREMY (*off stage*)
> I'm sorry, Maude!

MAUDE, *startled, breaks off her reading, and looks up from her typescript.* JEREMY *comes onto the stage. He is carrying* PENNY's *hat.*

> JEREMY
> I'm terribly sorry to interrupt your reading, Maude, but there's a bit of an emergency. (*He turns to face the*

audience and holds up the hat) Has anybody seen Penny
Sewell?

Blackout.

Act One Scene Five. The same evening.

*The barn. It is dark outside and the interior is unlit. The outside door
opens and* LEO *enters. He switches on the light, which reveals*
PENNY *asleep on the sofa.* LEO *freezes momentarily with surprise,
then moves quietly across to the sofa. He bends over* PENNY. *She
stirs slightly.*

LEO
Hey, Goldilocks.

LEO *shakes her gently.* PENNY *opens her eyes, gasps and sits up.*

LEO
Who's been sleeping on *my* couch?

PENNY
Oh, I'm sorry. Ever so cheeky of me to come in here,
but I wanted to be sure to see you. (*Yawns*) I must
have dropped off.

LEO
People have been wondering where you were.

PENNY
I didn't have any appetite for dinner.

LEO
Or for Maude's reading?

PENNY
Somehow I couldn't face it. She's so clever, I knew it
would only depress me more. Is it over?

LEO
I guess so.

PENNY
Was it terribly good?

LEO (*shrugs*)

If you like that kind of thing. Comedy of manners plus love interest plus a little gynaecology. What are you depressed about?

PENNY

What do you think?

Pause.

LEO

I can't take back what I said just to make you feel better.

PENNY

I'm not asking you to. I want you to tell me how to *write* better.

LEO

Oh.

PENNY

You told me earlier what I was doing wrong. I understand that, I think. Now I want to know how to do it right.

LEO (*slowly*)

You want me to tell you how to produce literary works of enduring value?

PENNY

Please.

LEO *shakes his head.*

PENNY

I know it's not a simple matter.

LEO

You bet your sweet – bet your life it isn't.

PENNY

But you *are* a teacher of creative writing.

LEO

I offer criticism. What my students do with it is up to them.

Act One Scene Five

>PENNY
>But surely you must have some advice, some hints, some tips.

LEO *stares at her for a moment.*

>LEO
>Care for a drink?

>PENNY
>No, thank you.

LEO *goes to sink unit and pours himself a scotch.*

>LEO
>Okay. I'll tell you how to write. I'll give you the magic formula.

PENNY *sits up expectantly. She takes from her handbag a small notebook and pencil.* LEO *takes a slow sip of his drink.*

>LEO
>Repetition and difference.

>PENNY
>What?

>LEO
>It's all a question of striking the right balance between repetition and difference.

>PENNY
>Sorry, I don't understand.

>LEO
>Imagine a text that was all repetition, that consisted of just one word, endlessly repeated. *Love, love, love, love, love, love, love, love, love, love, love, love, love,* and so on, for two hundred and fifty pages.

PENNY *laughs.*

>LEO
>Or: *Depression, depression, depression, depression, depression, depression, depression, depression, depression, depression, depression . . .*

PENNY

Stop! It's unbearable.

LEO

Exactly. Beckett came pretty close in some of his later work, but even he can't get away with just repetition. There must be difference as well. But imagine a text, that was *all* difference. A text that never used the same word twice, a text that introduced a new character, a new topic, a new storyline, in every sentence. Like, er . . .

LEO (*drinks, thinks*)

'*Jake was a tough cowboy . . . She went waterskiing every summer . . . If only I had remembered to fill up with gasoline before I tried to rob the bank . . . the dwarf said to himself.*' Er . . .

PENNY

You said 'I' twice.

LEO

So I did.

PENNY

And 'the'.

LEO

Right. It's hard to avoid. You can't have a text that's all difference, any more than you can have one that's all repetition. So you see, the whole secret of writing well, is knowing when to repeat yourself and when to differ from yourself.

PENNY

And how do you know *that*?

LEO (*shrugs*)

I've no idea. It's a mystery.

PENNY (*deflated*)

You're teasing me.

LEO

No, I'm not. It's something that comes unbidden, like grace . . . Look, I'll give you an example. In the

45

winter of 1981, I went to Poland, just before the
military takeover and the suppression of Solidarity.
There were terrible shortages of food and ordinary
things that we take for granted, like batteries, light
bulbs, soap. After I got back home, I became obsessed
with the idea of this guy who goes to Poland with a
suitcase full of soap, which he uses like currency, to
obtain services and favours, especially sexual ones. He
uses the soap to pay prostitutes. He does kinky things
with them, with the soap. I started writing the story,
but I couldn't see what the point of it was, or how it
could end. It was all soap and sex, soapy sex. I
abandoned the story, put it away, forgot all about it. A
few weeks ago I dug it out again, and as I was reading
through it, I suddenly flashed on why the guy was
doing this crazy stuff. Which is to say, why I had
fantasised him doing it. He's Jewish, you see, like me.
My family came from Poland, originally. There's a
long history of persecuting Jews in that part of the
world. Russians, Germans, Poles – antisemitism is
about the one thing they have in common. Through
the soap, by humiliating Polish *shiksas* with the soap,
my character's trying to take revenge, exact
reparation. His relatives would've been gassed in what
they thought were shower-rooms, and their corpses
boiled down to make soap. As soon as I saw that, I
knew that the story would end with the guy going to
visit Auschwitz and realising what he's doing, and
what it's doing to him. Soap, you see, had become a
kind of pun, a serious pun. Repetition and difference
compacted together. Bingo!

PENNY
Gosh!

LEO (*grins*)
Go thou and do likewise

PENNY
But what shall I write about?

LEO
I can't tell you that! Rewrite your novel.

PENNY
You said it wasn't worth going on with.

LEO
It wasn't so bad. There were touches. But there was
too much difference in it. It didn't rhyme – you know
what I mean?

PENNY
What touches?

LEO (*thinks*)
The image of the kids' toys scattered in the garden,
like the aftermath of an accident. That was striking. I
don't know what it was doing in the piece, but in itself
it was striking . . .

PENNY *makes a note.* LEO *tries to change the subject.*

LEO
How old are your children?

PENNY
I don't have any.

LEO (*surprised*)
You don't have children?

PENNY
No, Graham and I tried for years, but I kept on having
miscarriages.

LEO
That's tough . . . Why don't you write about that?

PENNY
Oh, no.

LEO
Why not? That's where your image of the toys comes
from, after all.

PENNY
Is it?

LEO
It's an image of loss, bereavement.

PENNY

I couldn't write about that. It's too private. Graham
wouldn't like it. Mother would have kittens.

LEO

Your mother-in-law?

PENNY

No, my mother. Graham's an orphan.

LEO

So you don't have a mother-in-law?

PENNY

No.

LEO

Do you have a job?

PENNY

Yes. I'm a primary-school teacher.

Pause, while LEO *digests this information.*

PENNY

I don't know what my headmistress would say, either.

LEO

Look, if you're going to worry about other people's
feelings, you might as well forget the whole idea of
being a writer.

PENNY

But supposing it were published. What would people
think?

LEO

What they always think, if they know the writer
personally. That the story is totally autobiographical.
You just have to remember that you're not writing for
your family, or your friends, or your employers, but
for readers, people to whom you are just a name on the
spine of a book.

The outside door opens and MAUDE *enters. One of her shoes and the
hem of her skirt are wet. She pulls up in surprise on seeing* PENNY.

MAUDE (*to* PENNY)
Oh! So you turned up? Are you all right?

PENNY
Quite all right, thanks. But you're wet.

MAUDE
Yes.

PENNY
I'm sorry I missed your reading.

MAUDE
You didn't just miss it, dear, you silenced it. (*She sits down and takes off her wet shoe*) Where were you?

PENNY
Here.

MAUDE
Leo found you here?

PENNY *nods*.

MAUDE (*to* LEO)
You didn't think to tell Mrs Sewell we've all been searching the river for her.

PENNY (*looking from one to the other*)
What?

LEO
I'm afraid it slipped my mind.

PENNY
Why the river?

LEO
Somebody found your hat on the river bank. It was feared you might have tried to drown yourself because I was unkind about your imagery this afternoon.

PENNY
But that's absurd!

LEO
That's what I said.

       PENNY

I did go for a walk by the river this afternoon. I must have left my hat down there.

       MAUDE

Yes, well, I think you'd better go back and call off the search party. I gave up when I nearly fell in the water myself.

       PENNY

Oh dear. I'm awfully sorry.

       LEO

It was my fault, Maude. We got talking.

PENNY *puts her notebook into her handbag and prepares to leave.*
MAUDE *wipes the mud off her shoe.*

       PENNY (*to* LEO)

I'd better go. Thanks for the advice. It was fascinating.

       LEO

Okay. (*He escorts her to the door*) Tell me, what kind of wallpaper do you have in your bedroom?

       PENNY (*puzzled*)

Here?

       LEO

At home.

       PENNY

We don't have any wallpaper. It's all white walls.

       LEO

You know, Penny, I think you may be a writer after all. I really believed in that wallpaper.

PENNY *smiles, and goes out.* MAUDE *watches this parting between*
LEO *and* PENNY *with an unfriendly, possibly even jealous
expression. As* LEO *shuts the door after* PENNY, *she turns her back
on him.*

       LEO

Maude! I'm sorry.

MAUDE (*coldly*)
I hope I didn't interrupt anything.

LEO
What's that supposed to mean?

MAUDE
I was just wondering why you seem suddenly to have
become a charismatic teacher, after two days of bored
indifference to the students. I thought perhaps the
wide-eyed innocent type appealed to you.

LEO
Don't be ridiculous. Let me fix you a drink.

MAUDE
No thank you, I'm going to bed.

MAUDE *goes to the stairs and ascends them in the course of the
ensuing dialogue.*

LEO
I'm sorry about your reading. I was really enjoying it.

MAUDE
Is that why you kept yawning?

LEO
It was hot in there. You could read another time.
Tomorrow – before me. I'll speak to Jeremy about it.

MAUDE
Please don't trouble yourself.

MAUDE *goes into her bedroom and shuts the door. The telephone
rings twice and stops.*

LEO (*calls up the stairs*)
Sounds like Henry's logging in, Maude.

LEO *goes over to phone and turns up volume control.*

HENRY'S VOICE
. . . there's a lot of white foam coming out of the
back of the dishwasher – can that be right? I wasn't
sure how much soap powder I should use and I
couldn't get the little box thing to shut, I don't know

> whether that had anything to do with it . . . But what
> I wanted to know is whether it's still under
> guarantee, I can't remember when we bought it . . .

LEO *looks up at* MAUDE*'s door.*

> LEO *(shouts)*
> Yeah, it's Henry. Want to take it? *(To phone)* Sorry
> Henry, she's pissed off. Won't speak to either of us.

LEO *turns off sound.*

Blackout.

Act One Scene Six. The following evening.

LEO *is seated in spotlight, facing the audience, exactly like* MAUDE
*in Act One Scene Four. He holds a yellow ringbinder containing a
typescript.*

> LEO
> This is a short story that I started several years ago,
> but only finished quite recently. It's called 'Soap'.
> *(Clears throat)* 'Soap.' *(Reads.)*

> Irving Zimmerman arrived in Warsaw with two
> medium-sized suitcases. One suitcase contained his
> clothes and lecture notes. The other was full of soap.
> Toilet soap. Palmolive, Lux, Camay – the basic
> American drugstore range, plus some imported soaps
> from England and France: Pears, Imperial Leather,
> Roger et Galet, Chanel, special handmade *trompe l'oeil*
> soaps in the form of fruit – apples, lemons, bananas;
> and soap from healthfood stores containing
> macrobiotic wheatgerm, almond oil and coconut milk.
> The customs officer sneezed in the powerful gust of
> perfume that came from this suitcase when
> Zimmerman opened the lid.

> 'Why are you bringing these?' said the customs officer,
> pointing to the soap.

> 'Gifts,' said Zimmerman.

'Why are you coming to Poland?'

'To lecture on American literature,' said Zimmerman. 'The United States Information Service sent me.'

The customs official was sufficiently impressed to wave him through. Zimmerman slipped him a bar of Oil of Ulay. 'For your wife,' he said.

The USIS officer who had briefed him in Chicago before his trip had given Zimmerman a list of commodities he should be sure to take with him because they would be unobtainable in Poland: torch batteries, toothpaste, coffee, soap. 'Coffee and toilet soap would make acceptable gifts,' he added. Also barter, Zimmerman thought to himself. He went shopping for soap.

That first evening in Warsaw Zimmerman attended a cocktail party at the US Cultural Attaché's apartment, with a bar of Pink Camay bulging each pocket of his suit. He offered one to a plump, blonde lady agronomist from Lublin. She looked somewhat surprised, but slipped it dextrously into her purse, and, when they parted, rewarded him with a smacking kiss. He imagined her rushing home to take a bath with his soap, and found the thought arousing.

The Attaché gave Zimmerman dinner and delivered him to his hotel, the Europejski, a faded monument to pre-war bourgeois luxury. In the marble-floored, art-deco lobby, unaccompanied women wearing hats sat under the potted palms and crossed their legs invitingly. One of them came boldly up to Zimmerman as he collected his key from the clerk, and pretended to know him. 'Hallo,' she said, in English, linking her arm with his.

'How many *zlotys*?' said Zimmerman.

'*Zlotys* no good,' said the girl. 'Twenty dollars.'

'How much soap?'

They agreed on three bars. Upstairs in his room, she took off her hat and most of her other clothes, and lay down on the bed.

'Let's take a shower together first,' said Zimmerman. He fetched a lemon-shaped tablet of soap from his suitcase. 'Don't worry,' he said, tossing it in his hand. 'This won't count as one of the three. I might even let you keep it.' He had thought of a way to do this. The girl giggled and went readily enough into the bathroom.

Stripped, in the perfumed steam of the shower, she was pink and spotty and overweight. He soaped her all over, feeling her nipples spring to life under his slippery fingers. She moaned with unsimulated pleasure as he lathered her mousy quim. She squirmed on his index finger like –

LEO *looks up as if distracted by a disturbance in the audience. He mimes watching somebody getting up and walking out. The sound of a door banging shut at the back or side of the auditorium. After a momentary pause he continues reading.*

She squirmed on his index finger like a hooked fish. Then he bent her over the side of the tub and buggered her with the soap. She squealed as he rammed it into her. Zimmerman had never done anything like this before. He felt enormously excited. Uplifted. Then –

LEO *breaks off again and mimes watching another person or persons walking out. The sound of the door slamming again.*

LEO
Does anyone else want to leave?

Evidently several persons do. The door slams once, twice more. LEO *considers, closes his ringbinder, and walks off the stage in disgust.*

Blackout.

Act One Scene Seven.
The same evening, a few minutes later.

The barn. LEO is sitting or lying sulkily on his bed. JEREMY is talking to him through the open door of the bedroom. MAUDE is observing with a certain detachment from the armchair. She is sipping a glass of white wine – the bottle is open on the sink unit.

JEREMY
It was just a few of the older people . . . The others are dying to hear the rest of the story.

LEO
No way.

JEREMY
Maude! Do help me persuade Leo to go back.

MAUDE
Would that be a good idea?

LEO comes angrily to the doorway of his room.

LEO (*to* MAUDE)
You approved of the walkout, then?

MAUDE
Of course not. But I did wonder whether that story was quite suitable for reading aloud to an audience that included a retired schoolmistress from Ilfracombe and a bank manager and his wife from Solihull . . . Some of our students have led rather sheltered lives, you see, Leo.

LEO
You can say that again.

MAUDE
Sodomising prostitutes with bars of soap may be all part of life's rich tapestry for you, but to the English middle classes . . . If it happens, they would prefer not to hear about it.

LEO
Exactly! And that's what's wrong with the English
novel. It's middleclass, middlebrow and middleaged.
It draws the curtains on reality and retreats into a cosy
drawing-room where the most exciting thing that can
happen is a menopausal widow having one drink too
many.

Pause. JEREMY *looks nervously from* LEO *to* MAUDE. MAUDE
extends her empty glass to JEREMY.

MAUDE
Could I have another drink, Jeremy?

JEREMY *brings wine bottle to fill* MAUDE's *glass and leaves bottle
on coffee table.*

MAUDE
Thank you.

JEREMY
I'd better go and tell the others the reading is over.

Silence as JEREMY *leaves, closing the door behind him.*

MAUDE
I hope you're not going to sulk. After all, we do expect
the students to accept criticism.

LEO
That wasn't criticism, it was a knee-jerk reaction by
frightened little minds.

MAUDE
All right, let me give you some criticism, then. Let me
try and articulate what they may have been reacting
against. Not just the sex, but the sexism.

LEO (*groans*)
Oh, no!

MAUDE
Oh yes! It wasn't just the elderly and infirm who
walked out, you know. So did some of the younger
women.

LEO (*with a trace of anxiety*)
Not Penny?

MAUDE
No, not Penny.

LEO
Look I've had feminist criticism up to here. Every
feminist in America has been kicking my ass for the
last two decades. There's nothing you could tell me
from that angle that I haven't heard already.

MAUDE
Then why do you go on doing it?

LEO
Doing what?

MAUDE
Abusing and humiliating women in your fiction.
'Ramming into them. Making them squeal.'

LEO
That was my character.

MAUDE
I thought everything one wrote came out of oneself,
ultimately.

Pause.

LEO
Look, all right, I admit that I'm fascinated by sex as a
power struggle, a struggle for dominance, with
violence at the heart of it, violence and tenderness
strangely entwined. Maybe that's a kind of source of
imaginative energy for me, like the core of a nuclear
reactor, white hot, deadly in itself, but a source of
terrific energy if controlled, cooled. That's what style
is to me. A coolant. That's why I write and rewrite
and rewrite.

MAUDE
'Soap' didn't seem particularly cool to me.

57

LEO
You can't judge a story by an extract.

MAUDE
You mean, Zimmerman becomes a reformed character
in the end?

LEO
Yeah, he meets a radical feminist who convinces him
he should cut off his balls.

MAUDE
I suppose he visits an extermination camp, Auschwitz
or somewhere, and has a spiritual illumination.

LEO, *stunned, turns to face* MAUDE.

LEO
How did you know that?

MAUDE
You mean I guessed right?

LEO
How?

MAUDE
Oh, you don't need to be clairvoyant to work it out.
Poland – Jews – soap . . .

LEO (*clutching at a straw*)
Penny told you!

MAUDE (*genuinely puzzled*)
Penny? How would she know? Oh! You mean you
confided the ending to her last night?

LEO, *plainly shaken, goes into his bedroom and fetches his yellow
ringbinder. He begins to leaf through his story.*

MAUDE
She's been burbling on all day about how inspiring her
lesson was. That's how she refers to it – her 'lesson'.
As if she were back at school. There's something
fundamentally immature about that young woman,
don't you think?

MAUDE *pours herself another drink, rather carelessly. She is just a little intoxicated.* LEO *continues to peruse his manuscript.*

> LEO
> Penny's all right. I tried to discourage her, but she came back fighting. I respect that.

LEO *sits down at the table and takes out a pencil from his pocket. He begins to make emendations to his manuscript.*

> MAUDE
> You know, your speech is absolutely saturated with imagery of combat.

> LEO (*preoccupied*)
> Is it?

Pause.

> MAUDE
> What are you doing? Rewriting your story?

> LEO
> Making some adjustments.

> MAUDE
> What kind of adjustments?

> LEO
> I think it should be raunchier.

MAUDE *laughs.*

> MAUDE
> While you were reading about Mr Zimmerman and his lady of the night, I couldn't help thinking of a scene in one of my own novels. *Fine Lines.* Have you read it, by any chance?

> LEO
> No, I don't think so.

> MAUDE
> The heroine, she's called Anna, discovers that her husband is having an affair with her best friend. She arranges to meet the best friend's husband in a park one day to discuss the matter. There's a violent

rainstorm and they both get soaked. As the park is near Anna's home, she invites Robin – that's the name of the best friend's husband – back to dry off. They're both shivering with the cold and the wet, so the first thing they do is have a stiff brandy each. Then they decide that they should have a hot bath to avoid catching cold. But there's only one bathroom in the house. Well, to cut a long story short, they end up having a bath together. She scrubs his back and he scrubs hers. They play with the children's bath toys. They shampoo each other's hair, and squirt each other with the shower nozzle. They have terrific fun. It's like a return to childhood. They rub each other down with hot towels. Then they get dressed and Robin leaves. They don't make love or anything. Yet it has been almost as good as making love for both of them.

LEO
Does Robin get an erection?

MAUDE
I don't know. I didn't say.

LEO
If Robin didn't get an erection, he was either impotent or gay.

MAUDE
He was neither.

LEO
Then they would have made love. Your scene is phoney. You wrote it with your eyes shut.

Pause, as MAUDE *decides not to take offence.*

MAUDE
It's interesting, isn't it, how the sex passages in men's books are always terribly detailed in a clinical sort of way about the private parts, what they look like and which bit goes where. Whereas with us, it's all rather vague visually. There's more emphasis on sensation, and emotion.

LEO

Most women, in my experience, don't believe their cunts are beautiful.

Beat. MAUDE *is both shocked and aroused by this statement.*

LEO

That's why they keep their eyes shut when they write about sex.

MAUDE

I see. Well, now we know.

Pause. MAUDE *pours herself another glass of wine.* LEO *continues to work on his manuscript.*

MAUDE

Have you ever, what's the word, resorted to prostitutes?

LEO (*looks up*)

Why do you ask?

MAUDE

It's none of my business, of course.

LEO

No, it isn't.

MAUDE

But I'm just curious. The whole transaction is so unimaginable.

LEO

I should have thought it was pretty straightforward.

LEO *resumes work on his manuscript.*

MAUDE

But it's just about the most intimate thing you can do with another person, isn't it? Taking off your clothes, lying down together, flesh to flesh. It must be extraordinary doing it with a total stranger, off the street.

LEO

The girl does it because she wants the money and the

guy does it because he wants to get laid. A lot of
marriages are based on the same principle.

MAUDE

But is there no caressing first – when you go with a
prostitute, I mean? No love talk? No tenderness?

LEO

Sure. But you pay extra for that. (*He looks up*) So I'm
told.

LEO *begins setting up his word processor.*

MAUDE

Working late?

LEO

Maybe. Depends how it goes.

MAUDE

Well, I won't distract you any longer. (*Drains her glass
and gets a little unsteadily to her feet*) I wonder if it's
always *just* for money.

LEO (*distractedly*)

What?

MAUDE (*musingly*)

Prostitutes. I wonder if they don't sometimes . . .
enjoy it.

The preoccupied LEO *does not respond. He taps impatiently on the
keyboard.*

LEO (*to computer*)

Come on, come on! You can do better than that.

MAUDE

Well, goodnight.

LEO

Goodnight.

MAUDE *ascends the stairs, goes into her bedroom, takes off her
clothes and puts on her dressing-gown. She comes downstairs again,
carrying spongebag. Meanwhile,* LEO *takes off his jacket, and starts
working on the revision of his story.* MAUDE *goes into the bathroom,*

leaving the door ajar. The sound of a shower running, faintly at first, then gradually amplified, overwhelms the tapping of LEO's *keyboard.* LEO, *momentarily distracted, glances up, then returns to his work. Wisps of steam begin to escape from the bathroom door.* LEO *turns round slowly and looks in the direction of the bathroom. He gets up and moves hesitantly towards the bathroom door. The significance of its being left open hits him. He makes a gesture of exultation towards the heavens, and strides towards the bathroom. Just as he reaches the door the telephone rings twice.* LEO *stops, looks back at the telephone, gives a shrug, and turns back to enter the bathroom. The threshold is filled with diffused steamy light.*

Curtain.

End of Act One.

ACT TWO

Act Two Scene One. The following afternoon.

The barn. SIMON *is standing beside the trestle table, reading* LEO's *story in its yellow ringbinder, turning the leaves rapidly. A soft Italian leather overnight bag lies on the floor at his feet.* SIMON *is in his early thirties, dressed in loose, trendy, all-black cotton clothes, and has an expensively styled haircut. He is good-looking in a slightly Mephistophelian way. As he reads, he takes a sip from a glass of whisky on the table beside him. The telephone rings and stops after two rings.* SIMON *locates the answerphone and turns up the volume.*

> HENRY'S VOICE
> **. . . it's an awful bore, Maude, but it looks as if Suki is pregnant. I've no idea who the father might be, have you? But, er, don't worry. Everything is under control. Goodbye.**

There is an electronic beep signalling the end of the message. SIMON *raises an eyebrow, shrugs, switches off monitor, and carries on reading. After a few moments he looks up and glances in the direction of the door as if he has heard something. He puts the ringbinder on the table, picks up his bag, and saunters to another part of the room. The outside door opens and* MAUDE, *wearing a light summer jacket or cardigan, comes in, taking off sunglasses as she does so.*

> MAUDE
> Simon! You're early.

> SIMON
> I decided to drive down. Steve Rimmer lent me his Porsche while he's on tour in Japan.

MAUDE *offers her cheek to be kissed.*

> MAUDE
> Nice to have friends so rich, and so trusting.

SIMON
Oh, Steve and I go back a long way. I used to cover
his gigs when he had a heavy-metal band called The
Pain Threshold. And before that we were at
Cambridge together. How are you, anyway?

MAUDE
Fine, thanks.

SIMON
How's the course going?

MAUDE
Well . . . you know Maurice is ill and Leo Rafkin has
come in his place?

SIMON
Yes. I have an awful feeling I wrote something rather
uncomplimentary about him once.

MAUDE
You did.

SIMON
Perhaps he's forgotten.

MAUDE
He hasn't.

SIMON
Ah. Oh well. How are you getting on with him?

MAUDE *goes to sink, fills kettle and switches it on.*

MAUDE
It was difficult at first. I can't say it's been dull. Tea?

SIMON
Thanks. You know, originally Jeremy asked *me* to be
the other tutor on this course.

MAUDE
Yes, I suggested it.

SIMON (*surprised*)
Did you?

MAUDE

Yes.

SIMON (*unsure how to interpret this information*)
I didn't know. Otherwise I might have agreed.

MAUDE (*giving nothing away*)
What a pity.

SIMON

I did it once before, and vowed never again. So I settled for the visiting writer slot.

The door opens abruptly, and LEO *comes in, at first seeing only* MAUDE.

LEO

Maude! Where have you been? I've been looking all over – (*He sees* SIMON *and stops. He looks displeased.*)

MAUDE

Leo, I believe you've met Simon before.

SIMON

Once, ages ago. Michigan, wasn't it?

LEO

Chicago. I promised myself the next time I met you, I'd punch you in the nose.

SIMON

Really? What did I do to deserve that?

LEO

You wrote a very offensive article about me, in a magazine.

SIMON

Did I? Most of my articles seem to offend somebody. I'm afraid I have a deep streak of offensiveness in me.

LEO

I'm not going to argue with that.

SIMON

Can I take it that you aren't going to punch me on the nose, either?

LEO *goes across to the sink unit without answering.*

> SIMON
>
> I would like to know. Otherwise I shall spend the rest of the day in suspense.

LEO *inspects the whisky bottle, which is almost empty.*

> SIMON
>
> Yes, I did help myself to a drink. But don't worry, I've got a full bottle of Johnnie Walker in the Porsche. (*To* MAUDE) It does a hundred and twenty without even trying. Six-speaker audio system. You've no idea how much better the Pet Shop Boys sound at a hundred and twenty miles per hour.

> MAUDE
>
> Who are the Pet Shop Boys?

> SIMON
>
> Really, Maude! Haven't your children educated you at all?

> MAUDE
>
> Henry won't let them play their records on his hi-fi. They have to listen in their bedrooms.

> SIMON
>
> With the volume turned down so low you can't hear any bass. I know, I know. By the way, have you got a pet called Suki?

> MAUDE
>
> No, an *au pair* girl. Why?

> SIMON
>
> Ah. Well, she's pregnant.

> MAUDE
>
> *What?*

> SIMON
>
> Somebody just left a message on the answerphone to that effect. Your husband, I presume.

MAUDE *hastens to phone, and dials.*

SIMON (*to* LEO)
How's the course going, then?

LEO
It's hard to tell when the students have no natural
aptitude for it.

SIMON
Don't be too sure about that. Some interesting writers
have been started off by the Wheatcroft.

LEO
Who, for instance?

SIMON
Well, me for instance.

MAUDE (*re-dialling*)
I didn't know you'd been a student here, Simon.

SIMON
Oh, yes. When I was eighteen. I wrote a complete
novel in four days.

LEO *whirls round to stare at* SIMON.

MAUDE
Simon! You dreadful liar! You've heard Jeremy tell
that story and you've stolen it.

SIMON
No, it was me. I was truanting from school. Enrolled
under a false name.

MAUDE *looks searchingly at him.*

MAUDE
I just don't know whether to believe you or not.
You're so horribly plausible.

MAUDE *puts the phone down.*

SIMON
That's why I'm a writer, no doubt. Couldn't you get
through?

MAUDE
No, engaged.

SIMON
Are you worried about this girl?

MAUDE
Well of course I'm worried. If she *is* pregnant. We've had a false alarm with an *au pair* before.

SIMON
I see.

SIMON *saunters over to the table on which* LEO's *computer is set up and taps on the keyboard.*

SIMON (*to* MAUDE)
Does this little gadget belong to you, Maude?

MAUDE
Good heavens, no. It's Leo's.

LEO
And I'd appreciate it if you wouldn't touch it.

SIMON *lifts his hands from the keyboard with an exaggerated gesture.*

SIMON
Sorry! It wasn't switched on.

MAUDE
Even so, you have to be careful with those things. One hears the most frightful stories of whole books being swallowed in a single gulp, because someone pressed the wrong key.

LEO
You'd have to be really dumb to do that.

MAUDE
Well, I can hardly work a pocket calculator, let alone a word processor. But I'm surprised you don't have one, Simon. You're usually so with it.

SIMON
No, I depend on the good old-fashioned fountain pen, for drafts anyway. See this small callus on my finger? (SIMON *shows* MAUDE *his index finger*) Writer's corn. (*He goes over to* LEO) I don't suppose you've seen one

Act Two Scene One

of these before, Leo. Most Americans never learn how
to do joined-up writing, do they? (*He holds his finger up
at* LEO) Writer's corn. (LEO *ignores the finger, looks*
SIMON *in the eye as if he would like to hit him*) Comes in
handy for foreplay. (SIMON *moves his finger suggestively
in a rubbing movement.*)

> MAUDE
> Simon, don't be disgusting!

SIMON *returns to the table. His hand hovers teasingly over the
keyboard, fingers moving in the air.*

> SIMON
> I daresay it's only a matter of time before writing is
> fully automated in the States. (*To* LEO) Or can you
> already buy software that actually writes the stuff for
> you? Like a programme for writing the Great
> American Novel. What would it be called . . . ?
> 'MEGAWRITER,' perhaps.

> LEO
> Very witty.

> SIMON
> 'WANKSTAR' for *Penthouse* stories.

> MAUDE
> Shut up, Simon.

> SIMON
> And, of course, for the ever-popular story of Jewish
> hangups about sex and the Holocaust – 'SOFTSOAP'.

> LEO
> You asshole! Have you been reading my
> manuscript . . . ?

LEO *moves threateningly towards* SIMON, *who retreats, raising his
hands in a mock gesture of surrender.* LEO *picks up his yellow
ringbinder from the table.*

> SIMON
> Sorry! Is it not intended for publication?

LEO

I should have kept my promise to punch you in the
nose as soon as I set eyes on you.

LEO *pursues* SIMON *angrily.* MAUDE *steps between them.*

MAUDE

For heaven's sake, stop acting like children, both of
you.

There is a knock on the door and JEREMY, *looking slightly flustered,
comes in.*

JEREMY

Simon! How did you get here?

SIMON

By car.

JEREMY

You might have let me know. I've been to Wareham to
meet the London train.

SIMON

Sorry, Jeremy! It completely slipped my mind.

MAUDE

Really, Simon, you are the limit.

JEREMY

Never mind, at least you're here. I was beginning to
fear this evening would be another fiasco.

SIMON

Oh? What's been going on, then?

MAUDE

My reading was interrupted by a suicide scare, Leo's
by half the audience walking out.

SIMON

Sensational! Why did they walk out?

MAUDE

Oh . . . it's a long story.

LEO (*to* SIMON)

You just read it, without my permission.

SIMON
I see. Well, I didn't think it was *that* bad.

LEO *glares at* SIMON.

JEREMY (*to* SIMON)
Some of the students were a bit shocked. I hope you won't do anything too controversial, Simon.

SIMON
You mean, I can't read my harrowing story about bestiality among Dorset sheep-shearers?

JEREMY
No.

SIMON
Can I say 'fuck'?

JEREMY
I'd rather you didn't.

SIMON
Oh, come on, be reasonable, Jeremy!

JEREMY
English writers managed perfectly well without that word until 1961. I don't understand why they've become so addicted to it since.

SIMON
As a concise description of the sexual act, I find I can't improve upon it.

JEREMY
All I'm asking is that you exercise a little restraint. This course can't afford another *débâcle*.

MAUDE
Oh dear, I detect a note of reproach.

JEREMY
Well, I must admit that things haven't gone as well as I'd hoped . . . There have been some complaints from the students.

LEO
What complaints?

JEREMY

Well, that they can't find you when they want you.

LEO

Jesus Christ! We gave tutorials all morning. What more do they want?

JEREMY

Several of them were wandering about after lunch looking for you.

MAUDE

I went for a walk with Mr and Mrs Baxter. The bank manager and his wife.

LEO *looks at her in astonishment.*

JEREMY

Well, that was very nice of you, Maude, I'm sure, but I'm afraid the other students tend to get jealous at the slightest *hint* of favouritism.

SIMON

You should have taken them to the pub at lunchtime, and got them all pissed. It's the only way to get any peace here.

JEREMY

Simon, shall I show you your room? It's in the farmhouse.

SIMON

Oh, can't I sleep with the other professionals?

JEREMY

You know there are only two bedrooms here.

SIMON

I don't mind sharing with Leo.

LEO

I mind. (*He sees, too late, that* SIMON *is joking.*)

JEREMY

They're only single beds, anyway. You'll be more comfortable in the farmhouse.

MAUDE

Yes, Simon, and you can make up for our
delinquencies by being very matey with the students.

JEREMY *goes to the outside door and holds it open.* SIMON *picks up
his bag.*

SIMON

That's what worries me. They'll keep me up all night
with questions about narrative technique and how to
get an agent.

JEREMY

You've got a room to yourself.

SIMON *and* JEREMY *go out.*

LEO

You seem to know St Clair pretty well.

MAUDE

We meet occasionally at publishers' parties, literary
festivals, that sort of thing. A few months ago we
judged a book prize together.

MAUDE *goes to the telephone, dials.*

LEO

He's even more obnoxious than I remember.

MAUDE

You mustn't let him get under your skin. 'He only
does it to annoy, because he knows it teases.' (*Listens
to phone*) Damn, still engaged.

LEO

How come he's the visiting writer on this course? I
mean, what's he *written*? Apart from journalism.

MAUDE *re-dials.*

MAUDE

He wrote a novel, when he was just down from
Cambridge.

LEO

Was it any good?

MAUDE

Precocious. Outrageous. Poetic descriptions of
nosepicking and masturbation figured prominently, I
seem to remember. But undeniably amusing. (*She puts
down phone*) Would you believe it, all weekend
Henry's been phoning me about trivia, and now I
actually want to speak to him I can't get through.

LEO

Has he published anything else?

MAUDE

A book of essays. No second novel, though he's
supposed to be working on one, has been for years. He
does a lot of book reviews.

LEO

I know, I've read them. If he can't write a book
himself, he's sure going to make life difficult for those
who can.

MAUDE *goes to window near the outside door and looks out.*

MAUDE

I'm afraid Jeremy is disappointed with us.

LEO (*approaches her*)

Why should you care what Jeremy thinks? He's lucky
you set foot in this dump.

MAUDE

Well, I know, but . . . It's probably sheer vanity, but
I like to be liked.

LEO

Let me take care of that.

LEO *places a hand possessively on* MAUDE's *haunch. She glides
away.*

MAUDE.

I'm talking about moral approval. It's a legacy of my
schooldays. I don't want Jeremy to give me a bad
report.

> LEO
>
> Maude.

LEO *follows her, takes her arm and turns her to face him. He kisses her.* MAUDE *quickly frees herself from his embrace.*

> MAUDE
>
> Not now, Leo.

> LEO
>
> Why?

> MAUDE
>
> Students may come knocking on the door at any minute.

> LEO
>
> Let them knock.

> MAUDE
>
> Simon may come back. He won't bother to knock.

> LEO
>
> Let's go up to your room, then.

> MAUDE
>
> Don't be ridiculous! It's the middle of the afternoon.

MAUDE *picks up a stack of manuscripts from a chair and carries them to the coffee table, where she begins sorting through them.*

> LEO
>
> People have been known to make love in the middle of the afternoon.

> MAUDE
>
> In the privacy of their own homes, perhaps.

> LEO
>
> 'Privacy of their own homes'? What is this genteel crap, Maude? Come to bed.

> MAUDE (*protesting laugh*)
>
> No!

> LEO
>
> Last night was terrific, wasn't it?

MAUDE

I'm not sure I want to discuss last night.

LEO

But you don't regret it?

Beat.

MAUDE

No.

LEO

Well, then.

MAUDE

There's a time and a place for everything. Now is the
time for me to look at Mr and Mrs Baxter's
manuscripts.

MAUDE *opens a file with the air of a teacher about to do some
'marking'.* LEO *looks at her in bafflement.*

LEO

Why the hell did you go walking with those creeps this
afternoon?

MAUDE

They're a very nice couple. Mrs Baxter has written a
charming story about a little girl being evacuated in
the War.

MAUDE *holds up a sheaf of handwritten pages tied together with
lilac ribbon. Then she examines a black ringbinder.*

MAUDE

Mr Baxter's work in progress is not quite so
promising. *Murder on the Eighteenth Green.*

LEO

I don't get you, Maude. Last night you were like an
animal in heat.

MAUDE

I presume you mean to be complimentary?

LEO

A beautiful, desirable, naked animal. It was the most
exciting sex I've had in years.

> MAUDE (*reading manuscript*)
> Good!

> LEO
> Today you're back to the tight-assed English rose you seemed when you first arrived.

> MAUDE
> You certainly have a way with words, Leo. '*Go lovely tight-assed English rose . . .*'

There is a knock on the outside door.

> MAUDE
> Someone at the door.

> LEO (*intensely*)
> Look Maude, I've been going around all day rigid with desire. When are we going to do it again?

> MAUDE
> That depends.

Another knock on the door.

> LEO (*shouts*)
> Go away! (*To* MAUDE) On what?

MAUDE *goes to door.*

> MAUDE
> On lots of things. My mood. Your discretion. I wouldn't count on it.

She opens the door, calls and beckons.

> MAUDE
> Lionel! Come back! (*To* LEO) It's Mr Brigstock for you, Leo. He has a *very* big manuscript under his arm.

Blackout.

Act Two Scene Two. The evening of the same day.

SIMON, *in loose white shirt and black trousers, is seated in spotlight, facing audience, like* MAUDE *in Act One Scene Four and* LEO *in Act One Scene Six, but with a glass of wine on the table beside him. He holds a stack of large index cards in his hand, on each of which is written one of the numbered sections of his text. After finishing each section he pauses and places the relevant card face down on the table.*

> SIMON
> I'm going to read something I've been working on for some time, called *Instead of a Novel*.

He takes a sip of wine, then reads:

> *One. The Jacket.*
> The jacket is made of laminated paper printed in six colours. The front cover reproduces a painting in the style of Magritte, depicting a book held open by a pair of hands. The pages of the book are completely blank, and, mysteriously, the reader's thumbs, which should be holding the leaves down, have disappeared into the white hole of the absent text. The title, *Instead Of A Novel*, runs across the top of the cover in inch-high lettering, and the name, 'Simon St Clair', across the bottom, in one-and-a-half inch lettering. Underneath the name, in smaller letters of the same typeface, is the legend, 'By the Author of *Wormcasts*'. Printed on the inside flap of the cover is an enthusiastic description of the contents of the book, known in the trade as the blurb.

> *Two. The Blurb.*
> '*Instead of a Novel* is, literally, indescribable. Is it an ingenious game? A shocking confession? A trap to catch the unwary reader? A dazzling display of literary virtuosity? All these things, perhaps, and more. *Instead of a Novel* fulfils the promise of Simon St Clair's brilliant and acclaimed first novel, *Wormcasts*, and sets new standards for conceptual daring and technical innovation in contemporary writing.'

Three. The Photograph.
The photograph, in black and white, on the back of
the jacket, is by Iain McKell, reproduced by
permission of *The Face*, where it first appeared. It
depicts the author in a loose ankle-length topcoat of
creased grey cotton over matching baggy trousers,
designed by Katherine Hamnett. He stares sulkily into
the lens of the camera, leaning against a pile of
damaged and obsolete juke boxes, video games,
electric guitars and amplifiers, in some sordid corner
of a North London junkyard.

Four. The Biographical Note.
Simon St Clair was born in 1957, and educated at
Westminster School and King's College Cambridge,
where he gained a First in English, and edited an
alternative student newspaper called *Camshaft*. While
he was still an undergraduate he began his first novel,
Wormcasts, which was published in 1980 to widespread
acclaim. It won him a Somerset Maugham Award and
the Whitbread First Novel Prize. After holding
various editorial posts with *Time Out*, the *New Musical
Express* and the *Listener*, he became a freelance writer,
contributing reviews and articles to magazines and
newspapers on both sides of the Atlantic on literature,
rock music and other aspects of contemporary culture.
A collection of his essays entitled *Graffiti* was
published in 1985. Simon St Clair lives in London.

Five. From the reviews of 'Wormcasts'
'A new and exhilarating voice in contemporary British
fiction (dot, dot, dot) scintillating wit and corrosive
irony.' – *Observer*.

'Seldom have the pains – and pleasures – of
adolescence been described with such devastating
accuracy.' – *The Times*.

'The thinking man's Sex Pistol.' – *Guardian*.

'Possibly the most brilliant fictional debut of the
decade.' – *Time Out*.

SIMON *rolls his tongue in his cheek as if to suggest that he may have inspired this last tribute himself.*

> *Six. The Title Page.*
> INSTEAD OF A NOVEL. A novel. By Simon St Clair.

> *Seven. Facing the Title Page.*
> Other books by Simon St Clair:
> > *Wormcasts*
> > *Graffiti*

> *Eight. The Dedication.*
> To Julian, for whom it was all too much.

> *Nine. Acknowledgements.*
> To Faber and Faber Ltd for quotations from *The Waste Land* by T. S. Eliot. To Methuen & Co for quotations from *Winnie the Pooh*, by A. A. Milne. To EMI for quotations from *Wish You Were Here* by Pink Floyd. To the Cambridge Arts Cinema where I whiled away many pleasant afternoons as an undergraduate assimilating the repertoire of Godard, Fellini, Antonioni, and Hitchcock. To Amanda, Cheltenham Ladies' College and Newnham, who let me go the whole way with her after our first May Ball, or would have done if I hadn't been too drunk to perform. To Julian, who held my head as I puked into the baptismal font of the Catholic church in Hills Road on my way home, and recommended cocaine as a less bilious method of getting high. To Amanda, who gave me next Michaelmas term a second chance to have her, which I seized, and enjoyed sufficiently to repeat the exercise on many occasions, until one day she forgot to take her pill and got pregnant, and I wanted her to have an abortion, but she didn't want to, but allowed herself to be persuaded. To Julian, who borrowed from his father the money that paid for Amanda to have a quick and discreet operation in St John's Wood, after which she said she never wanted to see me again. To Julian, who nursed Amanda through her post-abortion depression so that she was able to sit

Finals, and himself in consequence only got a
middling Two One, instead of the First he was
expected to get, and so lost his chance of a Fellowship.
To Amanda, who sensibly married a lawyer from
Trinity and had three children in four years. To the
author of a Sunday Colour Supplement article entitled
'New Contenders for the Glittering Prizes', who
featured me as an up-and-coming literary genius, and
to the photographer who took such a ravishing picture
of me reclining in a punt in a white suit that they had
to put it on the front cover. To the literary editors of
London newspapers and magazines who subsequently
fell over themselves to offer me work. To Verity
Blackwell, genius among editors, who accepted
Wormcasts within days of my submitting it, and wisely
persuaded me to cut the scene in which the hero is
fellated by a strange nun in the London Planetarium
on the grounds that one could have too much of a good
thing. To all my friends and acquaintances in the
media, who ensured huge publicity and enthusastic
reviews for *Wormcasts* on publication. To Julian, who
wrote the only unfavourable, and only honest, review,
in a little magazine that nobody reads, for which I
stopped seeing him. To Amanda, who came to the
launch party for *Graffiti*, gushing thanks for the
invitation, and whom I fucked afterwards for old
times' sake. To Julian who turned up at my flat one
night, high as a kite on cocaine, and put his arms
round me, and kissed me on the mouth, and told me I
was the only person he had ever loved, and whom I
promptly threw out, quivering with righteous
indignation like an outraged Victorian maiden. To
Julian, who died two years' later, a heroin addict. To
all the publishers, literary editors, agents, PR men, PR
women, TV producers, radio producers, record-
pushers, chat-show hosts, party-givers, lunch-givers,
freebie-givers, whores of every sex and profession,
who have given me so many excuses to put off writing
this novel.

Ten. The Epigraph.
'What draws the reader to the novel is the hope of
warming his shivering life with a death he reads
about.'

– Walter Benjamin

SIMON *lays down the last card, looks up.*

> SIMON
> The rest of the book consists of two hundred and fifty
> completely blank pages.

Blackout.

Act Two Scene Three. The same evening.

The barn. MAUDE, *alone in the sitting-room, is speaking into the
telephone.*

> MAUDE
> . . . so I want you to take Suki *immediately* to Dr
> Walters, the number is on the kitchen noticeboard,
> and ask him to give her a test. There's no point getting
> in a flap until we know whether she's really pregnant
> or just panicking.

LEO *comes in, stops just inside the threshold on realising* MAUDE *is
on the phone.*

> MAUDE
> Call me back as soon as you've seen Walters. Goodbye,
> Henry.

MAUDE *puts down phone.* LEO *sits in armchair.*

> LEO
> You finally reached him?

> MAUDE
> No, I had to leave a message on *our* answerphone.
> Henry is being annoyingly elusive.

MAUDE *sits down on sofa.* SIMON *comes in carrying a full bottle of
whisky.*

Act Two Scene Three

> SIMON
> One bottle of Johnnie Walker. As promised.

SIMON *breaks the seal, goes to the sink unit and pours two drinks.*

> SIMON
> I must say I need this. I always feel the adrenalin seething through my arteries after a reading. (*To* MAUDE) Say when, Maude.

SIMON *pours a little water into* MAUDE'S *glass.*

> MAUDE
> When.

SIMON *goes across to* MAUDE *with two glasses. He gives one to* MAUDE *and retains the other.*

> SIMON (*with mock courtesy*)
> Leo – please help yourself.

LEO *goes to sink unit to pour himself a drink.* SIMON *occupies his seat.*

> MAUDE
> Well, you certainly gave the students something to think about, Simon. They were quite stunned.

> SIMON
> You didn't like it.

> MAUDE
> Oh yes! It was very interesting.

> SIMON
> Ah, 'interesting'. The adjective of last resort for the author's friends.

> MAUDE
> No, really, it was terribly clever. Was it true?

> SIMON
> True?

> MAUDE
> I know it's true about your going to Westminster and King's and writing *Wormcasts* and so on, but the story of Julian and Amanda, and the abortion. Is that true?

84

SIMON

Really, Maude, what a very improper question to ask a novelist. I'm surprised at you.

MAUDE

Oh, come off it, Simon!

SIMON

It's like asking a lady her age. Or whether she's reached the menopause.

MAUDE (*startled*)

Have you been reading *my* manuscripts as well?

SIMON

One of the students, a Mr Brigstock, gave me an account of your reading at dinner.

MAUDE

Oh.

SIMON

But where did you get that amusing idea of waiting for a hot flush before walking the dog?

MAUDE

A friend of mine.

SIMON

How is she going to feel when she reads about it in your next novel?

MAUDE

Not half so bad as Amanda will feel when she reads yours.

SIMON

Ah, but I haven't admitted that there was an Amanda.

SIMON *goes to sink unit to fetch bottle. He refills his glass and takes bottle to* MAUDE.

MAUDE

I bet there was . . . Come on, Simon, spill the beans. We're all writers here.

SIMON
Isn't the usual phrase, 'we're all friends here'?

MAUDE
I mean, we can trust each other.

SIMON
Can we? If I ever have children, which God forbid, I shall tell them: 'Never speak to strange novelists, and be even more careful with ones you know.'

SIMON *tops up* MAUDE's *drink and takes bottle to* LEO.

SIMON
You're very quiet, Leo. What did *you* think of my story?

LEO *drains his glass, snatches bottle from* SIMON *and pours himself a generous measure. He thrusts the bottle back into* SIMON's *hand.*

LEO
I thought it was horseshit.

SIMON
Ah. You wouldn't be a teeny-weeny bit biased, would you?

LEO
I admit that it had a certain documentary interest.

SIMON
Yes?

LEO
As a glimpse of the rotting corpse of English literary life.

SIMON
A lurid image. How much do you know about English literary life?

LEO
You only have to go to a few publishers' parties, read the book pages in the newspapers, to understand how it works. The log-rolling, the back-scratching, the back-biting.

SIMON (*ironically*)

Of course, you don't get any of that sort of thing in
New York, do you?

LEO

I don't live in New York. It's a bigger country –
writers are more spread out. The trouble with England
is that it's too damned small. Everybody has his hand
in someone else's pocket and his nose in someone
else's asshole. And another –

SIMON (*holds up his hand*)

Just a moment! Let me think if that is anatomically
possible.

LEO

Life is too easy for people like you, St Clair. You glide
effortlessly from prep school to Cambridge, from
Cambridge to London, without ever stubbing your toe
on reality. Everybody knows everybody else in the
charmed circle that runs the literary world. Nowhere
is it so easy to get launched as a writer. But there's a
price to be paid.

Pause.

SIMON

I know you're dying for us to ask you what it is.

MAUDE

What is it, Leo?

LEO

The dreadful thinness of contemporary British
writing. It's glib, lazy, self-satisfied prattle.

MAUDE

You can hardly call Simon's story self-satisfied.

LEO

It is, it is! He luxuriates in his own obnoxiousness. He
has orgasms of self-loathing. Don't let the
metafictional tricks fool you. That piece is nothing but
bad faith jerking itself off.

SIMON

Oh, I like it! 'Bad faith jerking itself off.' I shouldn't be surprised if I stole that from you one day, Leo.

MAUDE

What does 'metafictional' mean?

SIMON

It's a bit of American academic jargon, Maude. Remember, Leo works in a university English Department. He can't open his mouth to breathe without inhaling a lungful of words like *metafiction, intertextuality, deconstruction*. They dance like dustmotes in the air of American classrooms.

MAUDE

But what does it mean?

LEO

It means fiction which draws attention to its own status as a text.

MAUDE (*bored recognition*)

Oh, *that*.

Pause.

MAUDE

Could we do something other than talk shop for a bit?

SIMON

Like what, Maude? Do you want to play cards?

MAUDE

Of course not.

SIMON

Scrabble? Charades?

LEO

I thought you were already playing charades.

MAUDE

I mean talk about something other than writing.

SIMON

Ah. The trouble is that writing is the only

conversational topic the three of us have got in common.

MAUDE
It would help if we had some music. I must speak to Jeremy about getting a radio or a gramophone in here.

SIMON
Music?

MAUDE
Not your kind of music, Simon.

SIMON
What kind?

MAUDE
At this time of night, with whisky . . . Frank Sinatra.

SIMON
Sinatra? You surprise me, Maude. I would have guessed baroque chamber music.

MAUDE *smiles her Mona Lisa smile. The alcohol is beginning to work on her.*

MAUDE
Ah, I'm a woman of many surprises. Aren't I, Leo?

LEO *doesn't know how to react to this.* SIMON *glances quickly from one to the other, sensing some subtext. He goes across to the telephone and dials, without lifting the receiver.*

MAUDE
What are you doing, Simon?

SIMON
I can't guarantee Frank Sinatra, and it won't be the highest of fi, but there is a London number you can call to hear the Golden Oldie of the week.

MAUDE *gets up and goes over to phone to listen.* SIMON *turns up the volume of the answerphone. Sound of Phil Collins singing 'One More Night'.*

MAUDE
Simon! You're a genius.

SIMON
Poor Phil Collins – a Golden Oldie already. He only
recorded that in 1985.

MAUDE (*sways her hips*)
It's nice. Smoochy night-club music.

LEO *turns his back on the others as he refills his glass.*

SIMON (*to* MAUDE)
Why not?

SIMON, *with a gesture unobserved by* LEO, *invites* MAUDE *to
dance. She slides into his arms.*

LEO
I heard Sinatra in Vegas once.

MAUDE
Did you?

LEO
For a man with no voice he was a pretty good singer.

LEO *turns, stares in astonishment and with jealousy at* MAUDE *and*
SIMON *dancing almost cheek to cheek.*

SIMON
You know, the reason Leo is so hysterically critical of
the English literary world –

MAUDE
Leave Leo alone, Simon.

SIMON
No, listen. If we're talking about bad faith, let's
consider the typical American writer. Nine out of ten
work at a university. An entirely bogus academic
subject, called creative writing, has been invented to
provide jobs for them. Fat salaries, pensions, grants.
My God, the *grants*! I bet he's on one now.

LEO *is silent.*

MAUDE
You are, Leo, admit it. (*To* SIMON) He has a
Guggenheim.

SIMON
Ah!

MAUDE
He's writing a novel about the end of the Second
World War.

SIMON
Still? (*To* LEO) You were working on that when I
interviewed you, what, five years ago.

LEO *visibly struggles to control his temper.*

LEO
It's a long book.

SIMON
The *War and Peace* of our time? Do you think that's
really your *métier*, Leo?

LEO *strides across to the answerphone and turns off the
music.*

MAUDE (*disappointed*)
Oh!

LEO (*to* SIMON)
What d'you mean by that?

MAUDE *and* SIMON *separate.* MAUDE *picks up her drink and takes
up a position centre stage: in the struggle that follows she is spectator,
umpire and prize.*

SIMON
I've always thought of you as an essentially anecdotal
writer, Leo. What do you know about war?

MAUDE
Leo was in the paratroops, Simon.

LEO (*quickly*)
I never said that.

MAUDE
Oh, I thought you did.

SIMON

No, he spent his military service teaching illiterate army cooks how to read, didn't you, Leo?

LEO

Don't push your luck, St Clair.

MAUDE (*to* SIMON)

How did you know that?

SIMON

I always do my homework before an interview. That's why my subjects usually take offence afterwards.

LEO

What about you, St Clair? You win any combat medals?

SIMON

Oh, National Service was before my time, I'm glad to say.

LEO

But then you don't need much experience to fill two hundred and fifty blank pages.

SIMON

No, only courage.

LEO (*laughs scornfully*)

Courage?

SIMON

Yes, courage to ditch all the obsolete machinery of traditional realist fiction. All that laboriously contrived suspense and dutifully disguised peripeteia.

MAUDE

What's that?

SIMON

Reversal. Usually combined with anagnorisis, or discovery, as everyone who took the Cambridge Tragedy paper knows.

MAUDE

Well, I didn't take it. Give me an example.

SIMON

For example, Zimmerman's moment of truth at
Auschwitz, in Leo's story. Aristotle was very hot on
reversal and discovery. But they've rather lost their
cutting edge, now that every TV commercial has
them.

LEO

So what's the new literary technology? The do-it-
yourself postmodernist novel? Two hundred and fifty
blank pages for the reader to write his own book in?

SIMON

Why not?

LEO

Those cheap tricks only work once.

SIMON

Another reason why they require courage.
Experimental fiction burns its bridges behind it, while
the realistic novel goes trudging up and down the same
safe, boring old highway.

MAUDE

Well, *I'm* a realistic novelist, and not ashamed to say
so.

SIMON

Ah, there's a special dispensation for women novelists
of wit and sensibility, Maude. It comes down from the
sainted Jane. (*To* LEO) Austen, not Fonda.

MAUDE

Oh, well, I do adore Jane Austen.

SIMON

You remember what Sir Walter Scott said about her?
'The big Bow-wow strain I can do like any now going;
but the exquisite touch, which renders ordinary
commonplace things and characters interesting, is
denied to me.' Now you, Maude, have the exquisite

touch, but I greatly fear that Leo is going for the big
Bow-wow strain in his war novel, about a hundred and
fifty years too late.

LEO

What the fuck do you know about my novel, St Clair?

SIMON

Only that it's taking you an awfully long time. You
aren't blocked, are you?

LEO

No, I'm not blocked.

SIMON

If you are, I'd advise putting in a few sex scenes. They
seem to come easily to you. Or have you got too many
already, for a novel that's supposed to be about the
Second World War?

LEO

You really are an asshole.

SIMON

Another little-known fact about Leo, Maude, is that
he used to write jerk-off stories for skin magazines
under another name.

LEO

Who the hell told you that?

SIMON

As I was saying, I do my homework.

LEO

I'm not ashamed of it. I was working my way through
graduate school. I had a wife and a young kid to
support.

SIMON

How touching. Like a Victorian mother going on the
streets to feed her starving family.

LEO

I'm warning you, St Clair . . .

MAUDE
Simon, stop it.

SIMON
It left its mark, though, on your style, didn't it,
writing porn? How did that passage in your story go?
'He felt her nipples spring to life under his fingers . . .
she moaned with unsimulated pleasure . . .' I mean,
really!

LEO
That's it.

Enraged, LEO *strips off his jacket.*

MAUDE (*warningly*)
Simon!

LEO *squares up to* SIMON, *who makes no move to defend himself.*

LEO
Fight, you sonofabitch!

SIMON
I wouldn't dream of it.

MAUDE
For God's sake, Leo!

LEO *makes a sparring motion with his left fist and pokes* SIMON *in
the face.* SIMON *gives a moan and crumples to his knees, covering
his face with his hands.* MAUDE *hurries over to him.*

MAUDE (*to* LEO)
I hope you're proud of yourself.

LEO
I hardly touched him.

MAUDE
His nose is bleeding.

SIMON *straightens up, holding a handkerchief to his nose. The
handkerchief and his shirt are stained red. He gets slowly to his feet,
helped by* MAUDE.

MAUDE
Are you all right?

SIMON (*indistinctly*)
I bleed rather easily, I'm afraid. I was known as
Bleeder St Clair at school.

MAUDE
Poor Simon. Come into the bathroom.

SIMON
No, I must lie down with my head back.

MAUDE *guides* SIMON *to the sofa. He lies down with his feet up and
his head back, one arm trailing to the floor, and the bloody
handkerchief held to his face. There is a knock at the door. All
freeze, uncertain what to do. The knock is repeated, and the door
opens.* PENNY *appears on the threshold. She has a pink folder in her
hand.*

PENNY
Oh, excuse me. I just wanted to give something . . .
(*she sees* SIMON, *pauses*) . . . to Leo.

MAUDE (*hostess voice*)
Do come in.

PENNY *enters, looking between* LEO, MAUDE *and*
SIMON.

MAUDE
Simon has had a nosebleed.

PENNY
Oh dear . . . Is there anything I can do?

MAUDE
I don't think so.

LEO
What did you want to give me, Penny?

PENNY
This. (*Hands him the folder*) It's something I just
finished writing.

LEO (*does not look inside*)
Oh, right.

PENNY

It's something new. Not exactly what you suggested,
but similar.

LEO

I'll try and have a look at it. (*He puts it down*) Come by
in the morning, okay?

PENNY

What time?

LEO

Oh, uh, ten-thirty.

PENNY

Right. See you at ten-thirty. Goodnight, then. (*She
looks in* SIMON's *direction*) I hope your nosebleed heals
up, Mr St Clair.

SIMON *grunts an acknowledgement.* PENNY *turns to
leave.*

LEO (*to* PENNY)

What did you think of Mr St Clair's reading?

PENNY

Oh, it was very . . . interesting.

A groan from SIMON. PENNY *goes out, closing the door behind her.*
SIMON *slowly sits up, then stands up, feeling his nose in a gingerly
fashion.*

SIMON

It seems to have stopped. I need to wash.

MAUDE

I'll come with you. You don't want to start the
bleeding off again.

MAUDE *escorts* SIMON *to the bathroom. They go in, leaving the door
ajar.* LEO, *looking unhappy, sits slumped in a chair with his drink.
The door of the bathroom closes, softly, but with a perceptible click.*
LEO *spins round, stares at the bathroom door. There is a knock on
the outside door, and* JEREMY, *dressed in a corduroy jacket, enters
hurriedly, carrying a first-aid box.*

JEREMY (*looking round*)
Where's Simon? Penny told me he had a frightful nosebleed.

LEO
He's all right.

JEREMY
She said he was stretched out on the sofa like 'The Death of Chatterton'. I wonder what caused it?

LEO
Picking his nose.

JEREMY
What?

LEO
He banged into something.

JEREMY
Oh dear, I do hope he doesn't claim against the insurance. The premium is overdue. Where is he, anyway? I've got some gauze and cotton wool in here.

LEO
He's in the bathroom, cleaning up.

JEREMY *moves towards the bathroom.*

LEO
Maude's with him.

JEREMY *stops in his tracks.*

JEREMY
Oh, well, I'll just leave the box, in case he needs it.

LEO
You can go in.

JEREMY
No, it's all right. (*He puts the box down on the table and moves towards the outside door*) I won't disturb them.

LEO
Wait!

LEO *comes across to* JEREMY.

> LEO
> 'Disturb them'? What the hell d'you think they're doing?

> JEREMY (*titters*)
> I don't know, I'm sure.

JEREMY *moves towards the outside door.* LEO, *beside himself with jealous suspicion, grabs his arm and turns him round.*

> LEO
> But you do have some idea?

> JEREMY
> Would you mind letting go of my sleeve? (LEO *releases his grip*) The material creases rather easily. (*Smooths sleeve*) If you must know, I think she fancies him.

> LEO
> Maude fancies that wimp?

> JEREMY
> She has a reputation for collecting young writers, you know.

> LEO
> No, I didn't know.

> JEREMY
> Yes.

The bathroom door opens. JEREMY *starts guiltily, and moves away from* LEO. MAUDE *comes out of the bathroom. There is a smear of blood on her bosom.*

> MAUDE
> Oh, hallo, Jeremy.

> JEREMY
> I gather Simon's been in the wars. I brought the first-aid box over.

> MAUDE
> Thanks, but he seems to be all right now.

JEREMY
Oh, good.

MAUDE
He's just washing the blood out of his shirt.

LEO
Some of it seems to have rubbed off on you.

MAUDE (*looks down at her bosom*)
Oh, dear. Never mind, it's an old dress. I thought the reading went rather well, didn't you, Jeremy?

JEREMY
Yes, the students were intrigued. And the fact that Simon's piece . . . what was it called?

LEO
Confessions of an Asshole.

MAUDE
Instead of a Novel.

JEREMY
Yes. I think the very fact that it was incomplete, a kind of conscious failure, as it were, made it reassuring to them.

LEO *grunts derisively.*

JEREMY
It'll be interesting to see what they produce themselves, tomorrow evening. Well, goodnight.

MAUDE
Goodnight, Jeremy.

JEREMY *goes out, shutting the door behind him.*

LEO
I'm sorry, Maude.

MAUDE
Apologise to Simon, not me.

LEO
I hardly touched him. That wasn't the punch I promised him.

MAUDE

You mean you're going to have another try?

LEO

There's no satisfaction in hitting a wimp who won't
fight back.

MAUDE

I thought Simon was remarkably brave, as a matter of
fact.

LEO

Brave?

MAUDE

He didn't even flinch when you rushed up to him like
some great snorting bull.

LEO

Yes, I fell right into his trap.

MAUDE

What trap?

LEO

I made a fool of myself, and embarrassed you. I'm
sorry.

SIMON *comes out of the bathroom in time to hear this last phrase. He*
is stripped to the waist.

SIMON

If you're really sorry, Leo, you could make amends by
swapping rooms tonight.

LEO

Why?

SIMON

Maude thinks I might suffer some after-effects. She
wants to be on hand if I need help.

LEO *looks at* MAUDE.

MAUDE

I think it would be best.

> LEO
> Jeremy can take care of him.

> SIMON
> I don't think Leo is going to take a hint, Maude . . .

> MAUDE (*dissociating herself from the wrangle*)
> I'm going to bed.

MAUDE *goes to the staircase and begins to ascend it, watched by*
LEO.

> SIMON (*to* LEO)
> It's quite a nice little room in the main house. At the
> top of the second flight of stairs, on the left.

LEO *watches* MAUDE *reach the landing and go into her bedroom.*
SIMON *fetches the whisky bottle from the sink unit.*

> SIMON
> A nightcap before you leave?

> LEO
> I'm not leaving.

> SIMON
> Actually, it's not your room we need, Leo, or even
> your bed. It's your mattress.

> LEO
> Go to hell.

> SIMON (*sighs*)
> Very well, we'll just have to shift as best we can. I
> hope we don't disturb your sleep. (*Glances speculatively
> at door of* MAUDE's *bedroom*) It could be noisy. I'd
> heard that she rather fancied younger men, but I
> didn't know she was quite so . . . ravenous.

Taking the whisky bottle with him, SIMON *goes to the stairs,
humming 'One More Night'.*

> LEO
> Not just younger men.

SIMON *stops on the stairs, turns and looks down at* LEO.

SIMON
Did you say something?

LEO
I said, not just younger men. I had her last night.

SIMON
Really?

LEO
You don't believe me?

SIMON
Give me some details. Make it convincing.

LEO
In the shower. Covered with soap.

SIMON (*shakes head sceptically*)
Too derivative, I'm afraid.

SIMON *proceeds up the stairs.*

LEO
St Clair! I'm not bullshitting you!

SIMON
A little O.T.T., as we say in the trade. Goodnight,
Leo.

SIMON *goes into* MAUDE's *bedroom and shuts the door behind
him.* LEO *goes to the sink unit and leans against the counter,
trembling, undecided what to do. The sound of low, erotic laughter
from the room above.* LEO *goes quickly into his bedroom and
snatches up pyjamas, dressing-gown, sponge bag. He comes out of
his bedroom and strides towards the outside door. His eye falls on*
PENNY's *folder, and he checks and picks it up. He strides to the
door, opens it, turns back and addresses the bust of Aubrey
Wheatcroft.*

LEO (*to bust*)
And up yours, too.

LEO *goes out, slamming the door behind him.*

Blackout.

Act Two Scene Four. The following morning.

The barn. The sitting-room is empty. The outside door opens and
LEO *comes in, carrying his pyjamas, dressing-gown, sponge bag and*
PENNY's *pink folder. He puts the folder on the table. He takes the*
rest of the stuff into his bedroom, pausing on the threshold to register
surprise at the fact that his bed has been slept in, and the mattress is
in place. He comes out of the bedroom and goes to the table to pack
up his computer. The bathroom door opens and MAUDE, *in dressing-*
gown and carrying her sponge bag, comes out.

> MAUDE (*demurely*)
> Good morning.

LEO *does not reply. He takes the lead from the socket and begins to*
coil it.

> MAUDE
> No word processing today?

> LEO
> I'm leaving.

> MAUDE
> Oh? When?

> LEO
> As soon as possible.

> MAUDE
> The students will be disappointed if you're not here
> for the last evening.

> LEO
> Too bad.

> MAUDE
> Simon's gone.

Beat.

> I'm afraid we all behaved rather badly last night.

> LEO
> All of us?

MAUDE

Well, you did hit Simon in a rather unchivalrous
fashion.

LEO

And you?

MAUDE

And me? Oh, dear, yes. Well, I'm not normally as bad
as that, you know. It was Simon I was interested in
when I agreed to come on this course. Your standing
in for Maurice Denton was an unexpected distraction.

LEO

What about Henry?

MAUDE

Henry?

LEO

Doesn't he come into your calculations at all?

MAUDE

Oh, Henry has his adoring young women. He gives
them special coaching in his college rooms.

LEO

And you have your adoring young men?

MAUDE

Why shouldn't I?

LEO

It's just . . . Your novels are full of such fine moral
scruple.

MAUDE

That's a rather nice phrase. I must remember to
suggest it to my editor for the blurb of *Dissuasion*.

LEO

*Dis*suasion?

MAUDE

Yes, that's what I'm going to call my new novel. Lying
in bed this morning I suddenly thought of how to go
on with it.

LEO
Is that why you're so perky?

MAUDE
Am I? Then I expect it is. It's going to be a novel
about how young people are shocked if their parents
claim the same freedoms as themselves. Marion falls
for Hamish of course, but it turns out that he's
unhappily married to a Catholic who won't divorce
him, so they have to –

LEO (*interrupting her*)
Are your children shocked at the way you behave?

MAUDE
No, I'm very discreet. You do persist in reading fiction
autobiographically, don't you?

LEO
I have a naive, old-fashioned idea that there should be
some moral consistency between the life and the work.

MAUDE
I'll let you into a secret, Leo. I was a repressed,
unfulfilled young woman, just like my heroines, the
'sleeping beauties' as you call them. Married to the first
man I slept with, who happened to be my tutor. It was
years before I realised I wasn't the last of his special
tutees. I didn't have a lover till I was thirty-five.

LEO
You've been making up for lost time since then?

MAUDE
Perhaps. A few years ago I wrote a novel about a
woman's sexual awakening. It was quite explicit by my
standards. Even had erections in it.

LEO
What's it called?

MAUDE
It was never published. My editor advised me not to.

LEO
Why?

MAUDE

He said it didn't work. I think really he was afraid it
would upset my readership.

LEO

I'd like to read it.

MAUDE

I'm afraid I destroyed it. I went back to my sleeping
beauties, which everybody admits I do rather well.

LEO (*genuinely shocked*)

You should never destroy anything you've written.

MAUDE (*amused*)

Why not?

LEO

It's part of your life's work. Critics in the future will
have an incomplete picture.

MAUDE

Do you think people will be reading your books after
you're dead?

LEO

I wouldn't go on writing otherwise.

MAUDE

Really? I think that's rather noble. Personally I shall
be content if they write on my grave, 'She gave
pleasure to her contemporaries.' (*Yawns*) I must get
dressed. You know, I'm rather sorry you're leaving
early, Leo. I've enjoyed these arguments we've had
about writing and so on. So did Simon, I do believe.

LEO

That argument had nothing to do with ideas. It was
just a literary version of the old Oedipal two-step:
waste Dad and hump Mom.

MAUDE

If it's any consolation to you, he was rather a
disappointment in that department.

LEO
You mean he was impotent?

MAUDE
Oh no, not as consoling as that. But it was all over rather quickly.

LEO
That why he slept in my bed?

MAUDE (*reflectively*)
I'm not sure Simon really likes women. That's really what his story was about.

LEO
Who's reading autobiographically now?

MAUDE
Well, Simon did rather invite it, didn't he? That was part of the game.

LEO
Ah, yes, the game. The writing game.

MAUDE
You must admit Simon's rather clever at it. (*She moves towards the stairs*) You're sure you won't change your mind about leaving? Penny Sewell will be terribly disappointed.

LEO
You know that piece she gave me to read last night? It's very good.

MAUDE
Really?

LEO
It restored my faith in what I do for a living.

MAUDE
Well, there's an achievement for a little primary-school teacher.

LEO
It's such an incredible advance on the first piece she showed me.

MAUDE
I think you owe it to her to stay for the reading
tonight.

LEO *broods on this.* MAUDE *begins to ascend the stairs.*

MAUDE
Don't misunderstand me. My concern is purely for a
happy conclusion to the course.

MAUDE *goes into her room. Almost at once there is a knock on the
door.* PENNY *opens it and stands on the threshold.*

LEO
Oh, hi Penny. Come in.

PENNY
I know it isn't half-past ten yet, but somebody said
you were leaving.

LEO
I wasn't going to leave without giving you back your
piece.

PENNY
What did you think of it.

LEO
Sit down.

PENNY *sits.* LEO *picks up the pink folder, opens it and leafs through
the contents.*

LEO
I don't know quite how to say this.

PENNY
It's no good.

PENNY *holds out her hand for the manuscript.* LEO *retains it.*

LEO
It's very good.

PENNY
Really?

LEO

It's a terrific improvement on that other piece you showed me.

PENNY

Gosh. Thanks very much.

LEO

But.

PENNY

But what?

LEO

You're not quite there yet. Nearly, but not quite. One day you could be a writer, a real writer. But probably not with this book. Probably in the end it will be a near miss. You'll have to put it in a drawer and start another. And maybe another.

While LEO *is speaking,* MAUDE, *now dressed, opens the door of her bedroom silently, and stands at the threshold, listening to the conversation, unobserved by* LEO *and* PENNY.

LEO

If you can face that, you'll get a book published eventually. And you'll think that's the summit of your ambition achieved. Publication! Wow! But maybe your book won't be noticed much, or you'll get some hostile reviews, and you'll discover that just being published is not enough after all — you also want success. Acclaim. So it's back to the desk and the typewriter again. It's a hard, lonely road, Penny. You sure you want to go down it?

Pause. PENNY *reflects.*

PENNY

No.

LEO (*disconcerted*)

No?

PENNY

No. I don't want to go down it.

LEO

But you've got talent, you know. I mean it. What I said to you just now, I don't say to many students.

PENNY

Yes, I appreciate that, and I'm grateful. But coming on this course has sort of cured me of wanting to be a writer.

LEO

You make it sound like some kind of disease.

PENNY

Well, it is, isn't it? A sort of fever. I see it in the other students. The way they look at you and Maude and Simon . . .

LEO

What way?

PENNY

A kind of mixture of awe and envy, because you're all *published*. And their desperate yearning to be published themselves. It's eating them away from inside, like cancer.

LEO

That's because they haven't got any talent. You have. You could be like us one day.

PENNY

I'm not sure I want to be.

Beat.

I'm sorry. That's really rude of me.

LEO (*waves the apology aside*)
It's all right. But tell me why.

PENNY

Well, you don't seem to be very happy.

LEO

Happy?

PENNY

No. And there's a sort of jealousy between you all the time. When Maude did her repeat reading, I was watching you, and during your reading I was watching Maude, and last night when Simon was reading I was watching both of you. I noticed that whenever the rest of us laughed at something in the reading, the other one or two of you looked unhappy. The most you could do was to force a thin smile. It was as if you begrudged each other the tiniest success. And then I heard you complimenting Maude on her reading . . .

LEO

The world is full of insincere compliments, Penny.

PENNY

The infants' class isn't.

Beat.

It seems to me that writers are a bit like sharks.

LEO

Sharks?

PENNY

Yes. I read somewhere that sharks never sleep and never stop moving. They have to keep swimming, and eating, otherwise they would get waterlogged and drown. It seems to me that writers are like that. They have to keep moving, devouring experience, turning it into writing, or they would cease to be recognised, praised, respected – and that would be death for them. They don't write to live, they live to write. I don't really want to be like that.

LEO (*indicates folder*)

Why did you write this, then?

PENNY

I suppose you wounded my pride, what you said about my *Lights and Shadows* piece. I'm used to getting good marks, you see. I thought to myself: 'Dammit, I'll show him.'

LEO
And you did. (*Slaps folder*) This is the real thing.

PENNY
And I see how easily I could get addicted to that kind
of praise. So I'm going to stop now, while there's still
time.

PENNY *gets up to go.*

LEO
I'm sorry.

PENNY
No, *I'm* sorry – for having wasted your time. But I do
appreciate the trouble you took, really I do.

LEO *holds out the folder.*

LEO
Here.

PENNY
Oh, keep it. Or throw it away.

LEO
You're not going to read this tonight?

PENNY
No, I think I'll slip away before this evening. Goodbye,
and thanks.

LEO
Goodbye, Penny.

PENNY *goes out.* MAUDE *steps forward on the landing and begins to
descend the stairs.*

MAUDE
I do hope she remembers to take her hat with her.

LEO
Were you listening to that?

MAUDE
Mrs Sewell has hidden depths. Somewhat
sanctimonious ones, I'm bound to say.

LEO *looks defeated, deflated.*

> MAUDE
> Cheer up, Leo.

> LEO
> I don't like to lose a potential writer.

> MAUDE
> You mean you don't like to lose a protégée.

> LEO
> Is she right? Are we really such assholes?

> MAUDE (*considers*)
> I think she's right about us devouring experience.
> Once you identify yourself as a writer, you can never
> just live, simply. It's all potential material. I remember
> when my mother was dying, I was thinking all the
> time how I was going to write about it. But that
> doesn't mean that I didn't feel genuine pity and grief.
> It's the same with the rivalry. It's inevitable between
> writers, between artists of any kind, but it doesn't
> mean you can't be friends as well.

The telephone rings twice and stops. MAUDE *picks up the phone.*
LEO *begins to unpack the computer and set it up again.*

> MAUDE
> Hallo, Henry . . . Yes, it's me, live. Where have you
> been? . . . Oh . . . She isn't? Well, that's a relief . . .
> Yes, I hope she will . . . Tomorrow, I should think
> about noon – it's a three-hour drive . . . The course?
> Oh, quite well, I think. (MAUDE *catches* LEO's *eye*) It's
> been very . . . interesting . . . No, Maurice dropped
> out at the last moment . . . Somebody called Leo
> Rafkin . . . An American . . . Do you remember a
> book called *The Wise Virgin*?

> LEO
> *Wise Virgins*!

> MAUDE
> Yes, very nice. Rather serious. He thinks English
> writers prattle. I daresay he's right. Goodbye, Henry.

MAUDE *puts down the phone.*

> MAUDE
> You've decided to stay, then?

> LEO
> I guess so.

> MAUDE
> Good.

LEO *switches on computer.*

> MAUDE
> Don't you find it a nuisance, carrying that contraption
> around with you everywhere?

> LEO
> It's okay. I don't have to carry a bulky manuscript
> around any more. (*He holds up a 3.5in floppy disc
> between his thumb and forefinger*) My entire novel is on
> three of these discs. Eighty thousand words, to date.

> MAUDE
> Show me how it works.

LEO *inserts disc, taps keyboard.* MAUDE *looks over his shoulder.*

> LEO
> 'Get file. Name of file: Chap. One.' There it is.

> MAUDE
> Goodness, just like magic.

> LEO
> You can scroll through it like this. (*Taps key several times.*)

> MAUDE
> What do you do now?

> LEO
> Well, I could revise it. Or I could dump it.

> MAUDE
> Dump it?

> LEO (*taps keyboard*)
> 'Delete all.'

MAUDE (*laughs*)
It says 'Really?'

LEO (*taps*)
Y for 'Yes.'

MAUDE
It's all disappeared.

LEO
Yeah. (*Taps*) 'Get Chap Two.'

MAUDE
Where's it gone?

LEO
Down the tubes. (*Taps*) 'Delete all. Really? Yes.'
(*Taps*) 'Get Chap. Three. Delete all. Really? Yes.'
(*Taps*) 'Get Chap. Four. Delete all. Really?'

MAUDE (*alarmed*)
What are you doing?

LEO
What does it look like? (*Taps.*)

MAUDE
You're destroying your novel!

LEO (*taps*)
Yep.

MAUDE
But why?

LEO
I've lost faith in it.

MAUDE
You mean Simon . . . ?

LEO
No, not that asshole. Well, maybe he has something to
do with it. He was right about my being blocked.

MAUDE
You'll get over it. *I* just have.

LEO

No, this is chronic. It came to me while Penny was
talking: I'm writing this novel not because I have to,
not because I really want to, but because I think my
career needs a big book. That's why it's not working. I
think I've known that for a long time, really. (*Taps*)
'Chap. Five. Delete all.'

MAUDE

Don't!

LEO

Why not?

MAUDE

You'll regret it. You said you should never destroy
anything. What about posterity? What about the
critics of the future?

Pause, while LEO *seems to give this appeal serious consideration.*

LEO

I have backup files at home.

MAUDE *laughs with relief.*

LEO

Backup files and heaps of printout.

MAUDE *goes to the coffee table and picks up some students' files.*

MAUDE

So it's just a symbolic gesture. You really had me
worried.

LEO (*taps*)

No, not just symbolic. I need the disc space for
something new.

MAUDE *settles herself to work.*

MAUDE

Are you going back to writing short stories?

LEO

No. I thought I'd try a completely different form.

MAUDE (*abstractedly*)
Oh?

LEO
Yeah. (*Slyly*) I've just had a great idea for a play . . .

As the implications of this remark sink in, MAUDE *slowly turns her head and stares at* LEO.

Curtain.

The End.